SCHOLASTIC

Hot Topics

Rainforests

ages
5–11
for all primary
years

Peter Riley

◣ SCHOLASTIC

Book End, Range Road, Witney, Oxfordshire, OX29 OYD
www.scholastic.co.uk

© 2008, Scholastic Ltd

89   456789

British Library Cataloguing-in-Publication Data
A catalogue record for this book is available from the
British Library.

ISBN 978 -0439-94553 - 0

Printed in the UK by Belmont Press Ltd, Northampton

Text © Peter Riley 2008

The rights of Peter Riley to be identified as the author of
this work have been asserted by him in accordance with
the Copyright, Designs and Patents Act 1988.

Editor
Roanne Charles

Development Editor
Kate Pedlar

Project Editor
Fabia Lewis

Cover and inside illustrations
Laszlo Veres/Beehive Illustration

Photocopiable page illustrations
Colin Elgie

Model-making
Linda Jones

Polaroid photos
Linda Jones unless otherwise credited.

Revised cover design
Mark Bryan

MIX
Paper from
responsible sources
FSC® C015185
FSC
www.fsc.org

Contents

INTRODUCTION   4

PLANNING A PROJECT   6

THEME 1
What are rainforests?   8

THEME 2
Rainforest plants   16

THEME 3
Rainforest invertebrates   24

THEME 4
Rainforest vertebrates   32

THEME 5
Rainforest people   40

THEME 6
Disappearing rainforests   48

THEME 7
Endangered species   56

THEME 8
Rainforest benefits   64

THEME 9
Saving the rainforests   72

IMAGE © STOCKER, STOCK.XCHNG

Introduction

The *Hot Topics* series explores topics that can be taught across the curriculum. Each book divides its topic into a number of themes which are ordered sequentially to build up a firm foundation of knowledge and provide opportunities for developing a wide range of skills. Each theme provides background information and three lesson plans, for ages 5–7, 7–9 and 9–11. Each lesson plan looks at a different aspect of the theme and varies in complexity from a simple approach with younger children to a more complex approach with older children. There are also photocopiable sheets to support the lessons in each theme.

BACKGROUND INFORMATION

Each theme starts by providing information to support you in teaching the lesson. You may share it with the children as part of your own lesson plan or use it to help answer some of the children's questions as they arise. Information is given about the photocopiable sheets as well as the answers to any questions which have been set. This section also provides a brief overview of all three lessons to help you select content for your own sessions.

The lessons

A detailed structure is provided for lessons aimed at children who are in the 7–9 age range. Less detailed plans, covering all the essentials, are given for the lessons aimed at the other two age ranges so covering the entire primary age range.

Detailed lesson plans

The detailed lesson plans have the following format:

Objectives

The content of all lesson plans is focused on specific objectives related to the study of rainforests.

Subject references

All lesson plans show how they relate to specific curriculum-related objectives. These objectives are based on statements in the National Curriculum in England. They may be used as they are, or regarded as an illustration of the statements that may be addressed and help you to find others which you consider more appropriate for your needs.

Resources and preparation

This section lists everything you will need to deliver the lesson, including any photocopiables provided in this book. Preparation describes anything that needs to be done in advance of the lesson, for example, sourcing rainforest foods and products. As part of the preparation, you should consult your school's policies on all practical work so that you can select activities for which you are confident to take responsibility. The ASE publication *Be Safe!* (ISBN 0-863-57324-X) gives useful guidance for conducting safe science activities.

Starter

A starter is only provided in the more detailed lesson plans for ages 7–9. It provides an introduction to the lesson, helping the children to focus on the topic and generate interest.

What to do

This section sets out point by point the sequence of activities in the main part of the lesson. It may include activities for you to do, but concentrates mainly on the children's work.

Differentiation

Differentiation is only provided in the more detailed lesson plans for ages 7–9. Suggestions are given for developing strategies for support and extension activities.

Assessment

This section is only provided in the lesson plans for the 7–9 age range. It suggests ways to assess children, either through the product of their work or through looking at how they performed in an activity.

Plenary

This section is only provided in the lesson plans for the 7–9 age range. It shows how children can review their own work and assess their progress in learning about rainforests. It is not related to other lessons, but if you are planning a sequence of lessons you may also like to use it to generate interest in future studies of rainforests.

Outcomes

These are only provided in the lesson plans for the 7–9 age range. They relate to the general objectives. You may wish to add more specific outcomes related to the context in which you use the lesson.

Extension

This section is found in the lesson plans for 5–7- and 9–11-year-olds. It allows you to take the initial content of the lesson further.

Flexibility and extra differentiation

As the lessons in each topic are clustered around a particular theme, you may wish to add parts of one lesson to parts of another. For example, in Theme 3, Rainforest invertebrates, you may like to add part of Lesson 2, in which children make a flashing firefly, to Lesson 1, which deals with some rather large rainforest invertebrates. This will expand the children's work on minibeasts.

In the lesson plans for 7–9-year-olds, differentiation is addressed directly with its own section. In lessons for the other age groups, differentiation is addressed by providing ideas for extension work. The themes, however, are arranged so that you may also pick activities from the different age groups to provide differentiation. For example, in a lesson for ages 5–7 you may wish to add activities from the lesson for 7–9-year-olds in the same theme.

Planning a project

You may like to use the topic for a class or whole-school project culminating in a Rainforest Day. This will need considerable preparation, but the result could be a very memorable event! This section provides some suggestions for activities leading up to the day and for a programme of events.

The suggested activities are featured in or based on the lesson plans shown in the third column. Read through each lesson plan to work out how the activity can fit into the context of your Rainforest Day.

Times are given for guidance only. Depending on your circumstances, you may want to lengthen or shorten any activity.

Rainforest Day: ages 5–7
Preparation

● Make sure that you have covered all the preparation needed to carry out the lessons on Rainforest Day. If the children are to perform the rainforest song, raise and lower a rainforest, mime animals and bring on a large model Earth, as suggested on page 73, they need to be prepared well in advance of the day.

● If appropriate, send a letter home asking for parents or carers to help make rainforest costumes. This could simply be a T-shirt and shorts to represent indigenous people or shirts and trousers and wide-brimmed hats to represent explorers. If you feel that some children will not be able to bring a costume, collect some items that they could use. You may like to set up a display of books and posters showing rainforest people that parents and carers can look at for ideas.

● As a feature of the day will be a rainforest meal, it is important to mention this in the letter home. Suitable food and drinks are: chicken, banana, orange, mango, avocado, pineapple and tapioca, with still bottled water.

● The classroom needs to be set up as a rainforest as suggested in Theme 1, Lesson 1, with the animals in place for when the children to enter on Rainforest Day.

Ages 5–7		Activity	Lesson plan	Pages
MORNING	30 minutes	Making a model rainforest home	Make a yano Theme 5, Lesson 1	41, 45
	30 minutes	Performing experiments and add flowers to the rainforest	Leaves and flowers Theme 2, Lesson 1	17, 21
	30 minutes	Adding large minibeasts to the rainforest	Rainforest minibeasts Theme 3, Lesson 1	25, 29
	15 minutes	Miming the movements of rainforest vertebrates	Move like an animal Theme 4, Lesson 1	33, 37
	30 minutes	Making a model rainforest chinampa	Make a chinampa Theme 5, Lesson 2	42, 46
AFTERNOON	30 minutes	Sequencing rainforest destruction and make recycled paper	Timber! Theme 6, Lesson 1	49, 53
	40 minutes	Hearing a story about an orang-utan	Orang-utans Theme 7, Lesson 1	57, 61
	30 minutes	Final rehearsal and performance of 'Rescuing the rainforest'	Rescuing the rainforest Theme 9, Lesson 1	73, 77
	10 minutes	Performance of 'Rescuing the rainforest'. This may be done after a performance of 'Selling it off' by older children.	Rescuing the rainforest Theme 9, Lesson 1; Selling it off Theme 6, Lesson 2	73, 77; 50–51, 54–5

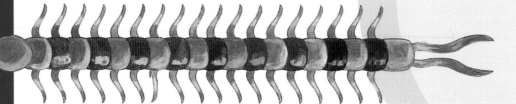

Rainforest Day: ages 7–9
Preparation

- If appropriate, send a letter home asking for parents or carers to help make rainforest costumes. This could simply be a T-shirt and shorts to represent indigenous people or shirts, trousers and wide brimmed hats to represent explorers. If you feel that some children will not be able to bring a costume, collect some items that they could use. You may like to set up a display of books and posters showing rainforest people that parents and carers can look at for ideas.
- The classroom needs to be set up as a rainforest as suggested in Theme 1, Lesson 1, with the animals in place for when the children enter on Rainforest Day.
- You could work on the Aztec calendar featured in Theme 5, Lesson 2 and count down the days to Rainforest Day in Aztec days.
- If the children are to perform the play in Theme 6, Lesson 2, they need to be prepared in advance.

Rainforest Day: ages 9–11
Preparation

- If appropriate, send a letter home asking for parents or carers to help make rainforest costumes. This could simply be a T-shirt and shorts to represent indigenous people or shirts, trousers and wide brimmed hats to represent explorers. If you feel that some children will not be able to bring a costume, collect some items that they could use. You may like to set up a display of books and posters showing rainforest people that parents and carers can look at for ideas.
- You may like to discuss with the children the decorating of the classroom to simulate a rainforest and use ideas from Theme 1, Lesson 1 and Theme 3, Lesson 1 to create a rainforest environment.
- If the children are to perform the play in Theme 6, Lesson 2, they need to be prepared in advance.

Ages 7–9		Activity	Lesson plan	Pages
MORNING	20 minutes	Colouring rainforest minibeasts and placing them in the classroom rainforest	Rainforest minibeasts Theme 3, Lesson 1	25, 29
	40 minutes	Making a model flashing firefly	Fireflies and crickets Theme 3, Lesson 2	26–7, 30
	30 minutes	Learning the differences between monkeys and apes	Monkeys and apes Theme 4, Lesson 2	34–5, 38
	40 minutes	Making a yano and a chinampa	Make a yano Theme 5, Lesson 1; The Aztecs Theme 5, Lesson 2	41–3, 45–6
AFTERNOON	40 minutes	Making masks and a video presentation about extinction	Animals at risk Theme 7, Lesson 2	58–9, 62
	40 minutes	Debating ideas for rainforest conservation	Good idea, bad idea Theme 9, Lesson 2	74–5, 78
	40 minutes	Final rehearsal of the play 'Selling it off'	Selling it off Theme 6, Lesson 2	50–51, 54–5

Ages 9–11		Activity	Lesson plan	Pages
MORNING	40 minutes	Investigating how seedlings grow and find light in a rainforest	Seedlings and light Theme 2, Lesson 2	18–19, 22
	40 minutes	Making a model flashing firefly	Fireflies and crickets Theme 3, Lesson 2	26–7, 30
	30 minutes	Exploring harmful invertebrates encountered on a jungle trek	Rainforest dangers Theme 3, Lesson 3	28, 31
	20 minutes	Discussing reasons for rainforest exploitation	Rainforest destruction Theme 6, Lesson 3	52
AFTERNOON	30 minutes	Debating the hunting of rainforest animals	The effects of poverty Theme 7, Lesson 3	60, 63
	40 minutes	Working out a strategy for saving the rainforest	Rainforest conservation Theme 9, Lesson 3	76, 79
	20 minutes	Final rehearsal of the play 'Selling it off'	Selling it off Theme 6, Lesson 2	50–51, 54–5
	10 minutes	Performance of 'Selling it off' to precede the song 'Rescuing the rainforest', performed by younger children	Selling it off Theme 6, Lesson 2 Rescuing the rainforest Theme 9, Lesson 1	50–51, 54–5; 73, 77

What are rainforests?

BACKGROUND

Rainforests are sometimes called jungles. This word comes from the Hindi *jangala*, which means 'wilderness' and is usually associated with the dense vegetation found at the edge of the rainforest, in a clearing or along a river bank. Inside the rainforest, dense vegetation at ground level gives way to a clear forest floor covered in dead leaves: the crowns of the trees prevent much of the light reaching the floor so few plants grow there. A rainforest has the following characteristics: many trees over 30m high; many climbing plants; many plants called epiphytes, such as orchids and ferns, which grow in leaf mould and soil on tree branches; many of the trees have buttresses on their trunks, which help to hold them up; rainfall is 200cm a year and at least 10cm a month.

The forests studied in this book are the tropical evergreen rainforests of the lowlands, especially in South America. Tropical rainforests are found around the equator. At other latitudes the Sun's rays cover a larger area of land due to the way the Earth curves. At the equator the surface offered to the ray is almost flat and the ray covers a smaller area so heats it more strongly, so giving a constantly hot climate. The hot air causes a high rate of surface evaporation. It also causes a high rate of transpiration (the escape of water from leaves). The water vapour rises in the currents of hot air. As it rises, it cools and forms clouds, which eventually release the water again as rain. Although the forest floor may have sparse vegetation, the amount of plant growth increases higher into the trees up to a tangle of branches, epiphytes and climbers. It may take a raindrop ten minutes to fall through the leaves to the forest floor.

THE CONTENTS
Lesson 1 (Ages 5–7)
Let's make a rainforest!
The children make trunks, leaves and wildlife to form a classroom 'rainforest'.

Lesson 2 (Ages 7–9)
A rainforest climate
The children compare how seeds germinate in classroom conditions and 'rainforest' conditions.

Lesson 3 (Ages 9–11)
Rainforests of the world
The children identify the countries in which rainforests are found.

Notes on photocopiables
Let's make a rainforest! (page 13)
A butterfly, a tree frog and a lizard are provided for the children to colour in, cut out and place in their classroom rainforest.

A rainforest climate (page 14)
These instructions show children how to carry out an investigation into plant growth involving a fair test.

Rainforests of the world (page 15)
Rainforests are located on the world map for the children to find out in which countries the rainforests are found.

IMAGE © EJBEVAN, STOCK.XCHNG

Lesson 1 Let's make a rainforest!

ILLUSTRATION © LASZLO VERES/BEEHIVE ILLUSTRATION

Objectives
● To use coloured pens creatively and scissors safely.
● To set up a rainforest scene.

Subject references
Art and design
● Record from first-hand observations and explore ideas.
(NC: KS1 1a)
● Try out tools and techniques and apply these to materials and processes.
(NC: KS1 2b)
● Represent observations and make images.
(NC: KS1 2c)
Science
● Recognise and compare main external parts of the bodies of humans to other animals.
(NC: KS1 Sc2 2a)

Resources and preparation
● Provide books showing rainforest scenes, butterflies, frogs and lizards.
● Each child or small group will need: a photocopy of page 13, coloured pens and crayons, scissors, large pieces of green paper to make leaves, pieces of wallpaper on which to draw and colour tree trunks.
● You will need: a globe and strip of green paper; (for the Extension) a selection of plants to set up a rainforest corner – Swiss cheese plant, urn plant and other bromeliads, philodendron, ficus, pitcher plant. You may like to refer children to the following website to experience how a rainforest looks and sounds at night: www.nationalgeographic.com/earthpulse/rainforest.

What to do
● Show the children some rainforest images. Note that the trees and leaves are much bigger than those in the local area. Explain that rainforests grow around the middle of the Earth where the weather is hot and wet. Wrap a length of green paper around the equator on a globe and tell the class that, from space, the rainforests make the Earth look like it has a green belt.
● Discuss with the children how they could make a wall of the classroom look like a rainforest using the large pieces of paper and rolls of wallpaper.

● Let the children draw and cut out large leaves on the green paper and tree trunks on the wallpaper. Explain that there is a huge number of different trees in a rainforest with colours ranging from black through shades of brown to white. Let the children colour the tree trunks. You may like to have some tree trunks with buttresses.
● The children could then help teaching assistants set up the trunks and leaves on the classroom walls.
● Show the children pictures of rainforest butterflies, frogs and lizards. Tell them that many frogs have poisonous skins that are brightly coloured to warn other animals of the danger. Let the children colour in, and then cut out, the creatures on the photocopiable sheet. Explain that they should colour both the top and underside of the butterfly then fold its wings so that they stick up.
● The children can then choose where to place their animals among the trunks and leaves.

Extension
Set up a corner with real rainforest house plants. Show the children the care labels and organise them to take turns at watering the plants. The soil of the pitcher plant will need to be kept moist.

Lesson 2 A rainforest climate

Objectives
● To understand why the Earth is hottest at the equator.
● To make a fair test to investigate the effect of rainforest conditions on plant growth.

Subject references
Science
● Know that the Sun and Earth are approximately spherical.
(NC: KS2 Sc4 4a)
● Ask questions that can be investigated scientifically and decide how to find answers.
(NC: KS2 Sc1 2a)
● Make a fair test.
(NC: KS2 Sc1 2d)
● Make systematic observations and measurements.
(NC: KS2 Sc1 2f)
● Use a table to communicate data.
(NC: KS2 Sc1 2h)
● Use observations and measurements to draw conclusions.
(NC: KS2 Sc1 2j)

Resources and preparation
● You will need: a globe, a torch, a piece of card with a small hole to make a light beam, books showing rainforest scenes, rainforest house plants as suggested for Lesson 1.
● Each child or small group will need: a photocopy of page 14, paper, pens, two plant pots filled with compost, up to 40 mustard seeds, a plastic jar (to fit over a plant pot), a measuring cylinder, space on a sunny window sill; thermometers (for more confident learners).

Starter
● Discuss that the Sun and Earth are spheres in space and the Sun releases energy as light and heat. Tell the children that this energy passes through space as rays, some of which strike the surface of the Earth.
● Explain that your torch represents the Sun, and the beam of light represents a ray of light and heat. Shine the beam on the equator of the globe and ask the children to note the size of the area illuminated. Now, without moving the position of the torch, shine the beam onto areas nearer the poles and let the children see that a larger area is illuminated. Tell the children that this difference is due to the curve of the Earth. At the equator, the Earth only curves slightly away from the Sun's rays.

This means that the full power of the ray shines on a small area giving it large amounts of light and heat. Further away from the equator, the curve is greater, so the ray must cover a larger area and each illuminated part receives less light and heat than at the equator. This is why the Earth is hottest at the equator.

What to do
● Tell the children that the heat in rainforest areas makes plants lose large amounts of water and any water on the leaves evaporates into the air. Explain that hot air rises and cools and when it does so, the water vapour condenses and forms clouds, which then release rain back onto the forests.
● Show the children a pot of compost and put a clear plastic jar over it, then explain that you can make rainforest conditions inside the jar and see how this affects plant growth. Can the children explain how they could investigate the effect of rainforest conditions on plant growth?
● Go through the photocopiable sheet with the children and compare their ideas with the suggested procedure.
● Let the children decide how many seeds they want to use. If necessary, guide them to use a large number of seeds to give a more accurate result.
● Also let them decide how much water to

give the pots, but tell them to check with you to ensure that they will not waterlog the compost.
- Ask the children to devise their recording tables on a separate piece of paper.
- The children should then place their pots on the window sill and observe them daily. They should see condensation running down the inside of the jar. They may find that the compost without the jar dries out a little and needs some extra water.

Differentiation
- Less confident learners should be able to count out the seeds and plant them, but they may need help in making the table and recording their observations.
- More confident learners could set up two pots of compost without seeds (again one to have a jar). They should place a thermometer in each pot so that the bulb touches the soil, and set up the pots on a sunny windowsill, with each thermometer's bulb shaded by a piece of cardboard. They could compare the temperatures of the air inside and outside the jar. Note: they should not remove the thermometer from the jar to read it.

Assessment
The children can be assessed on the number of seeds they select to germinate and grow,

the amount of water they choose to add, the construction of the table and the quality of their observations.

Plenary
- The children should look at the pots of other groups and then present and discuss their observations. They should conclude that the plants in the rainforest conditions grow faster.
- You might like to show the children some pictures of rainforest scenes and present them with a selection of rainforest house plants. The children could set up the plants around the classroom in accordance with their care labels and take turns at watering and observing them.

Outcomes
- The children understand why the Earth is hottest at the equator.
- The children can make a fair test to investigate the effect of rainforest conditions on plant growth.

IMAGE © DIALAVIEW, STOCK.XCHNG

Did you know?
It is hot and humid inside a rainforest, like a bathroom when someone has had a hot bath or shower.

Lesson 3 Rainforests of the world

Objectives
- To understand why the Earth is hottest at the equator.
- To identify countries where rainforests grow.

Subject references

Science
- Know that the Sun and Earth are approximately spherical. (NC: KS2 Sc4 4a)
- Investigate the effect of temperature on plant growth. (NC: KS2 SC2 3a)

Geography
- Use an atlas. (NC: KS2 2c)
- Find locations of places and environments. (NC: KS2 3b)
- To describe where places are. (NC: KS2 3c)

Resources and preparation
- You will need: a globe, a torch, a piece of card with a small hole to make a light beam, access to a street lamp, a ruler.
- Each child will need: pictures of rainforests, a photocopy of page 15, pens, an atlas. For the Extension: a globe, small pieces of green fabric and Blu-Tack® .

What to do
- Begin this lesson with the starter from Lesson 2 to explain how the spherical shape of the Earth contributes to the equator being the hottest region of the Earth.
- Remind the children of the effect of heat on plant growth from any earlier work that they have done on this topic.
- Then take the children outside and show them a lamp post. If it is about 8m tall, tell the children that many rainforest trees are five times that height and some can even be ten times that height.
- Point out that in the hot conditions of the rainforest, plants like bamboos can grow at a rate of 23cm per day. (Show this measurement on a ruler.)
- Take the children back to the classroom and let them look at some pictures of rainforests. Then issue photocopiable page 15 and the atlases. Ask the children to make a list of the countries that have rainforests in a) Central and South America, b) Africa, and c) South East Asia and the Australia region. Tell them that this information will be used later in connection with investigations into rainforest products.

Extension
Tell the children that the rainforests are sometimes described as a green belt around the centre of the Earth. Ask the children to assess the appropriateness of this description by taking a globe and sticking pieces of green material on the areas where rainforests grow.

IMAGE © EJBEVAN, STOCK.XCHNG

Theme 1 Let's make a rainforest!

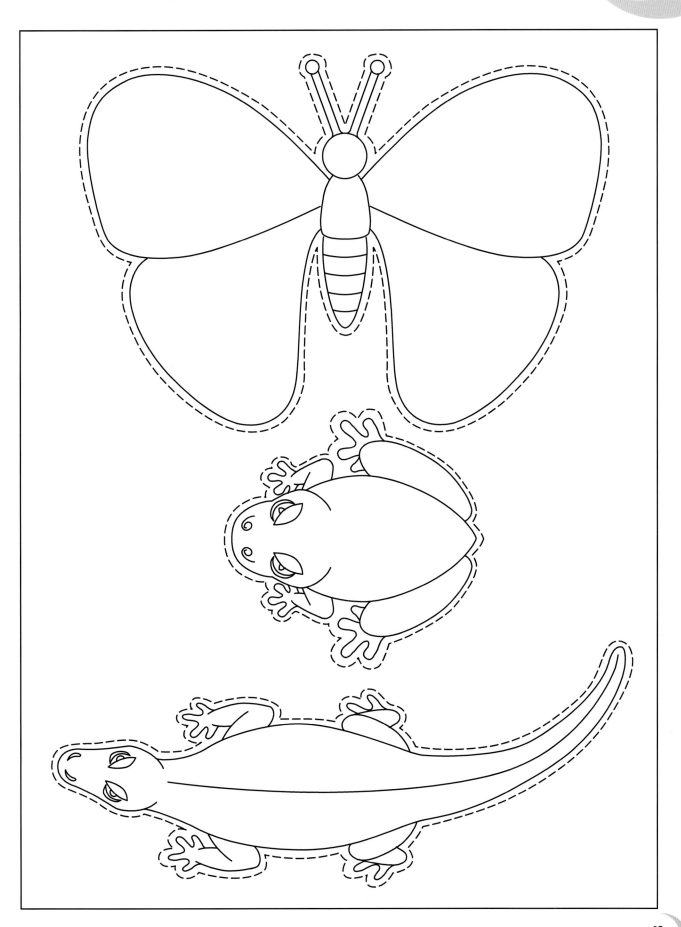

■SCHOLASTIC
www.scholastic.co.uk

Theme 1 A rainforest climate

1. Count out two groups of mustard seeds. Make sure you have the same number of seeds in each group.

2. Plant each group in a pot of compost.

3. Give the same amount of water to each pot.

4. Place a plastic jar over one plant pot.

5. Put both pots on a sunny windowsill.

6. Check each pot every day and record your observations in a table.

7. After two weeks, draw a picture of the plants in both pots.

Plants without jar

Plants with jar

Theme 1 Rainforests of the world

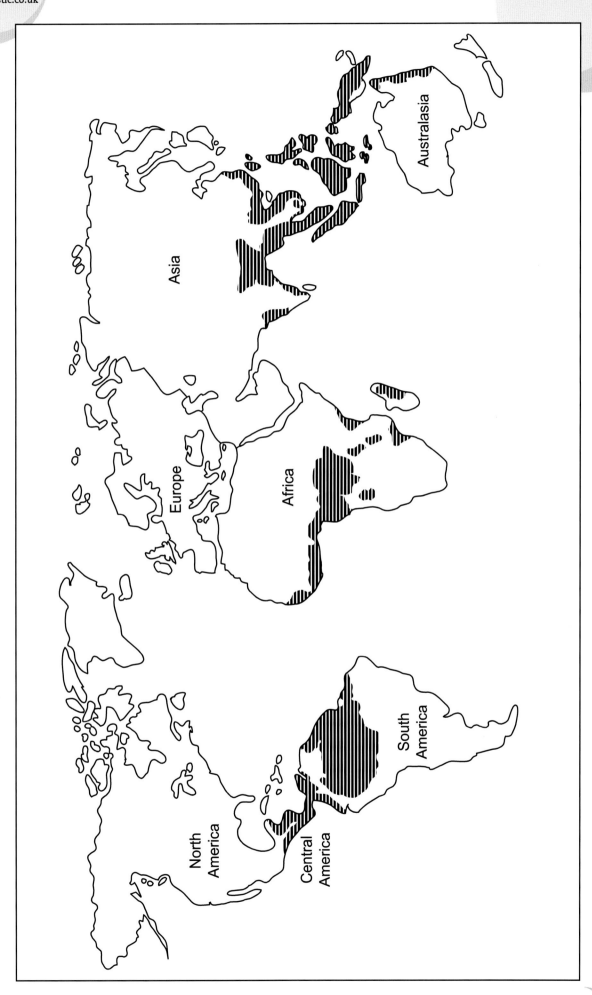

Asia

Australasia

Europe

Africa

North America

Central America

South America

Rainforest plants

BACKGROUND

Rainforest vegetation is divided into four layers: the undergrowth (from the forest floor to about 5m high); the understorey (from 5m to 20m); the canopy (from 20m to 30m) and the emergent layer (30m to 60m). Thick vegetation only occurs on the edges of clearings or on river banks where light can penetrate. Under the canopy, few plants grow in the dim light. The seeds of some plants wait in the soil for a clearing to develop before germinating and growing into the light. A clearing develops when one or more trees fall. A dead tree crashing down might take a few others with it. Some trees acquire so many epiphytes on their branches that they become top heavy, or a strong wind may bring a tree down.

Most rainforest plants are evergreen. It is very important that the leaves have clean, water-free surfaces to collect as much light as possible to make food. They have waxy surfaces, and some also form drops of water that flow easily over the surface and off the leaf. The waxy surface also prevents water getting inside the leaf and waterlogging the tissues.

Rainforest trees produce flowers and fruits on twigs, as trees in other habitats do, but some also produce bunches of flowers and fruits on their trunks. This is called cauliflory. These flowers produce a strong smell, which has been described as a mixture of sour milk and sweaty feet. This smell attracts bats, which feed on the nectar and pollinate the plants. The flowers are produced on the trunks so that bats can easily fly to them.

THE CONTENTS
Lesson 1 (Ages 5–7)
Leaves and flowers
The children investigate the effect of wax on water drops and the effect of a drip tip on clearing water from a model leaf. They make flower clusters to attach to their classroom rainforest.

Lesson 2 (Ages 7–9)
Seedlings and light
The children investigate the growth of seedlings without light then the effect of light shining from just one direction. They see if a plant can find its way to light when its path to the light is partially blocked.

Lesson 3 (Ages 9–11)
Pollination
The children read and answer questions on an account about bat and bird pollination.

Notes on photocopiables
Leaves and flowers (page 21)
This shows how to test the effect of wax on a surface and how to test the effect of a drip tip. It shows types of flowers that grow from tree trunks.

Seedlings and light (page 22)
This shows how to investigate the effect of light on plant growth.

Pollination (page 23)
This is an account of bat and bird pollination, with questions based on the text. Answers: 1) In the canopy; 2) Bees or bats; 4) Because of its scent of rotting meat; 5) They are red or orange and have no scent, while bat-pollinated flowers are cream or white and have a strong scent; 6) Sunbirds perch, while hummingbirds hover; 7) The flower is fertilised and produces seeds.

IMAGE © MOONCAT, STOCK.XCHNG

HOT TOPICS Rainforests

Lesson 1 Leaves and flowers

Resources and preparation
- You will need: pictures of rainforest plants or the plants from the classroom collection set up in Theme 1.
- Each child or small group will need: a photocopy of page 21, two pieces of newspaper about 10cm square and two pieces about 6cm square, a wax crayon, a teaspoon, a bowl of water, two pieces of waxed card (for example, from a box for chocolates) about 11cm x 4cm – one cut to a point as shown on page 21. For the Extension: coloured paper, pipe cleaners and sticky tape and/or other materials for tree-trunk flowers.

What to do
- Show the children some rainforest plants and point out that their leaves are shiny due to a thick coating of wax. The leaves have to keep the water out, otherwise the plant would die. They also have to get rid of water to maximise the amount of light that they get, especially if the water is dirty. Tell the children they are going to investigate the effect of wax on the surface of a newspaper 'leaf'.
- Issue page 21, the newspaper and crayons. Tell the children to colour one small square of newspaper with the crayon, then set up the squares of newspaper as shown on the sheet.
- Issue the spoons and water and ask the children to place a drop of water in the middle of each small square. The drop on the wax should be more rounded as the wax prevents it soaking into the paper.
- Ask the children what they think the paper under each square might be like, and look for an answer about the paper under the unwaxed square being wet and the other being dry. When they carefully move the squares they may find that their answers are correct, or that much less water has passed through the waxed square.
- Show the children some rainforest plants with drip tips. Now issue the two card leaves and ask the children to hold up each card at a slight angle and place a drip on each one. They should see how the water runs down the card and drips off it. Some water gathers at the bottom edge of the straight card; a much smaller amount is left on the card with a tip.

Extension
Consider how to make bunches of flowers to stick on the tree trunks in the classroom. Refer to the illustrations on the photocopiable. Let the children make flower bunches and stick them on their rainforest display.

AGES 5–7

Objectives
- To investigate the surface and shape of rainforest leaves.
- To show how and where some rainforest trees produce flowers.

Subject references
Science
- Recognise when a test or comparison is unfair. (NC: KS1 Sc1 2d)
- Make simple comparisons. (NC: KS1 Sc1 2h)
Art and design
- Record from first-hand observation, experience and imagination and explore ideas. (NC: KS1 1a)
- Investigate the possibilities with a range of materials and processes. (NC: KS1 2a)

PHOTOGRAPH © PETER ROWE

Lesson 2 Seedlings and light

Objectives
● To investigate the effect of light on seedling growth.
● To record observations.
● To use the results of investigations to explain how seedlings in the rainforest might grow.

Subject references
Science
● Know that it is important to test ideas using evidence from observations.
(NC: KS2 Sc1 1b)
● Make a fair test.
(NC: KS2 Sc1 2d)
● Use observations to draw conclusions.
(NC: KS2 Sc1 2i)
● Explore the effect of light on plant growth.
(NC: KS2 Sc2 3a)

Resources and preparation
Each child or small group will need: a photocopy of page 22, paper, pencils, four pots of germinated mustard seeds and a pot containing a germinated broad bean seed (the shoots of the seedlings should be visible above the surface of the compost), a box, a sunny window sill, two boxes with a hole cut in the side, black paint and brush, a shoebox, card, scissors, sticky tape; (for more confident learners) digital camera.

Starter
● Issue the photocopies of page 22. Talk about the arrangement of rainforest plants into layers, using the picture on the photocopiable to illustrate what you say. Tell the children that the rainforest floor is only exposed to light where it forms a river bank or when some of the tall trees fall down to make a hole in the layers and expose the forest floor – a clearing.
● Ask the children to draw a picture of the rainforest, using the illustration on the photocopiable sheet for guidance, but showing how a tall tree has brought some others down to expose the forest floor to light. Tell them that when they have finished

they will consider how plants react to various amounts of light.

What to do
● Begin by setting up the investigation shown in the second picture on the photocopiable sheet: set up two pots of seedlings, one in the dark and one in the light. The seedlings should be observed every day and watered as necessary. Let the children construct a table on a separate sheet of paper in which to record their observations. They should make qualitative observations, such as colour of leaf and stem, but some children might also want to measure the height of the stems.
● Now set up the investigation shown in the third picture: each pot of seedlings should be placed under a cardboard box, one with a gap on the right-hand side and one with a gap on the left-hand side. You might want to give the children boxes in which to make holes themselves, and some may elect to make large or small holes and decide where to make the hole. Alternatively, cut holes in the boxes before the lesson. When the children are making a table for their observations, you should

tell them that, this time, you want drawings showing how the seedlings grow rather than notes about colour or measurements. Observe the pots every day and water as necessary.

• The children could prepare the shoebox as in picture 4 during the lesson or at some time before. They should paint the inside of the box (including the lid) black, cut out the card baffles and paint them black too. They should cut a hole in the top of the box and, when the paint is dry, bend the baffle cards and stick them in place. The pot containing the bean seedling should be placed in the box and the box closed. Tell the children to make drawings of the bean seedling daily. The pot should be watered as necessary.

Differentiation

• Less confident learners will need help in constructing the boxes for the investigations shown in pictures 3 and 4. They may also need support in recording their observations.

• More confident learners may like to use a digital camera to record their daily observations, store them on a computer and arrange a photographic sequence showing the growth of the seedlings.

Assessment

The children can be assessed on the way in which they assemble the baffles in the shoebox and how they record all of their observations.

Plenary

• Tell the children that it is not completely dark on the forest floor, but it could be very gloomy. Ask them what they might expect to happen to seedlings, which need plenty of light, if they start to grow up from the forest floor. Tell them to use their results from the investigation shown in picture 2 to prompt their answer. (The seedlings would be long and spindly and weak, and eventually would die.)

• Ask the children what might happen if

a gap in the forest developed to the left or the right of where the seedlings were growing. They should use their results from the investigation shown in picture 3 to help them answer. (The seedlings would grow towards the light.)

• Now ask what might happen if a seedling had lots of leaves of other plants (from the fallen trees) above it. They should use their results from the investigation shown in picture 4 to help them answer. (The seedling would grow around the leaves in its way.)

Outcomes

• The children can perform investigations and record their results.

• They can use their results to explain how seedlings in a rainforest might grow.

PHOTOGRAPH AND POLAROIDS © HELEN TAYLOR

Lesson 3 Pollination

IMAGE © SCORNEJOR, STOCK.XCHNG; POLAROID © RZN, STOCK.XCHNG

AGES 9–11

Objectives
• To review pollination in the life cycle of a plant.
• To locate where different rainforest pollinators are found.
• To compare the structure of the rainforest with a local woodland.
• To realise that a rainforest is a very different place to a local woodland.

Subject references
Science
• Learn about pollination.
(NC: KS2 Sc2 3d)
English
• Use inference and deduction.
(NC: KS2 En2 2a)
• Obtain specific information through detailed reading.
(NC: KS2 En2 3c)

Did you know?
Figs are pollinated by wasp larvae that live in their flowers. They carry pollen away when they become adults.

Resources and preparation
• Each child will need: their copies of photocopiable page 15 completed in Theme 1, Lesson 3, a copy of photocopiable page 23, pens or pencils.
• You will need pictures of: rafflesia, a hummingbird, a sunbird, a bat feeding on a bat-pollinated flower; (for the Extension) a metre rule.

What to do
• Before this lesson, make sure that the children have studied the basic life cycle of a plant and parts of the flower and they understand that pollination is the transfer of pollen from the anthers of one flower to the stigma of another flower of the same species. The children should also know that fertilisation follows pollination and leads to the formation of seeds.
• Ask the children to tell you about the life cycle of plants and refer to those in the local area. Focus on the roll of bees and butterflies as pollinators and say that these creatures are also major pollinators in rainforests. Go on to tell the children that in the rainforests there are also other pollinators, and issue photocopiable page 23.
• Read the text with the children and show them your picture collection.
• Make sure the children have their own copies of page 15 from the previous lesson

and then let them answer the questions on page 23.
• Go through the answers and discuss how the rainforest is different from a local woodland that the children may know or have studied.

Extension
• Draw the layers of the rainforest on the board and include their respective heights (from the Background on page 16).
• Take the children to a local woodland and ask them to draw the layers: the ground layer (moss and short grass); field layer (taller plants such as nettles and ferns); shrub layer (such as holly bushes); and tree layer (from the height of the first branches up to the tree tops).
• Challenge the children to estimate the size of the tallest tree by putting a metre rule next to its trunk, standing some distance away so that a pencil held in an outstretched hand appears to be the same length as the metre rule, then moving the pencil up and counting out the lengths until the top of the tree is reached.
• Let the children use this method to see how high a rainforest tree of between 30m and 60m would be and compare it with the height of the woodland tree.

HOT TOPICS Rainforests

PHOTOCOPIABLE

Theme 2 Leaves and flowers

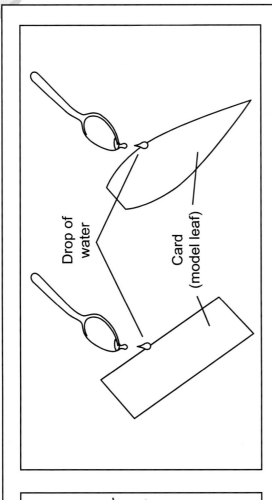

Drop of water

Card (model leaf)

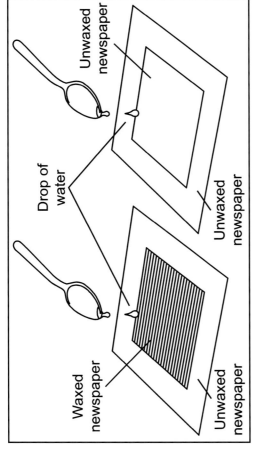

Drop of water

Unwaxed newspaper

Unwaxed newspaper

Waxed newspaper

Unwaxed newspaper

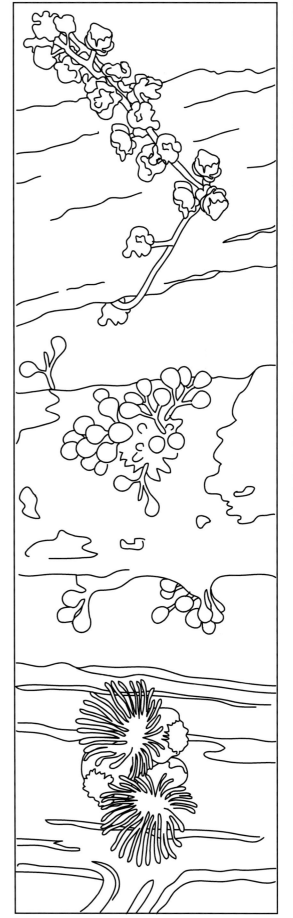

■SCHOLASTIC
www.scholastic.co.uk

Theme 2 Seedlings and light

1

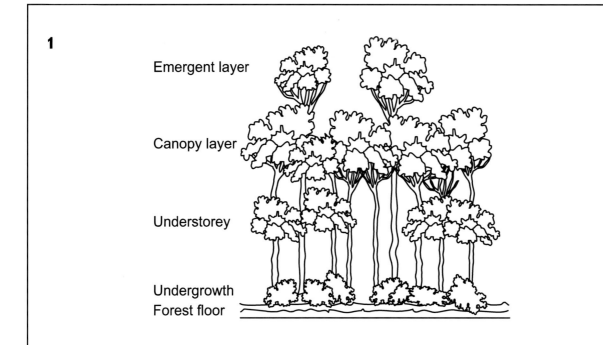

Emergent layer

Canopy layer

Understorey

Undergrowth
Forest floor

2

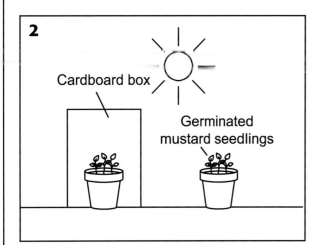

Cardboard box

Germinated
mustard seedlings

3

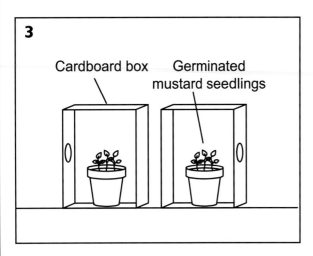

Cardboard box　　Germinated
mustard seedlings

4

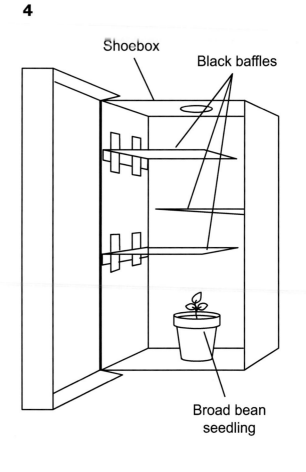

Shoebox

Black baffles

Broad bean
seedling

Theme 2 Pollination

Most rainforest plants produce their flowers in the canopy and are pollinated by insects such as bees. Some plants produce their flowers lower down and are pollinated by other animals.

On the forest floor grows a plant with the scientific name *rafflesia*. It has a flower that is 1m in diameter and produces a scent like rotting meat. This attracts flies which pollinate the flower. Rafflesia grows in the rainforests of Borneo and Sumatra and is also known as the stinking corpse lily.

Some rainforest plants are pollinated by birds. Many of them have red or orange flowers that do not produce a scent. In African rainforests, the flowers are pollinated by sunbirds. A sunbird perches next to the flower and probes into it with its long curved beak. As the sunbird sucks up the nectar, the feathers on its head become coated with pollen. In South American rainforests, hummingbirds pollinate flowers. These birds can beat their wings so fast that they can hover in front of the flower to feed. A hummingbird also has a long beak for reaching deep into the flower and as it feeds pollen grains cling to its head feathers.

Bats pollinate some of the rainforest plants that grow in South America, Africa and Australia. These plants produce white or cream flowers, which may be shaped like a trumpet or a shaving brush. They produce a strong scent similar to sweaty socks and sour milk. Some bats hover in front of the flowers then plunge their heads in to lap up the nectar. Other bats cannot hover, so they cling to the flower to feed. As all the bats feed their fur picks up pollen, which is carried to the next flower.

1. Where in the rainforest are most flowers found?
2. Name an animal that pollinates these flowers.
3. On your map of rainforests, mark the places where a) the stinking corpse lily, b) sunbirds, c) hummingbirds and d) pollinating bats are found.
4. Why do you think rafflesia is called "the stinking corpse lily"?
5. How are bird-pollinated flowers different from bat-pollinated flowers?
6. What is different about the way sunbirds and hummingbirds feed on nectar?
7. What happens after a flower has been pollinated?

Rainforest invertebrates

BACKGROUND

There is a huge number of different animals living in the rainforest. In order to study the many species of living thing, biologists divide them up into groups. The members of each group have certain similarities. One way of dividing up the animal kingdom is to split it into invertebrates (which do not have a skeleton of bone) and vertebrates (which do have a bony skeleton). Each group is then divided into smaller groups. Earthworms and leeches form a group called annelids, whose bodies are supported by water inside them. This 'water skeleton' is also found in another group, the molluscs, which includes slugs and snails. Many invertebrates have an external skeleton like a suit of armour. They include centipedes (one pair of legs per body segment), millipedes (two pairs of legs per body segment), insects (three pairs of legs) and spiders and ticks (four pairs of legs).

Rainforest insects take many forms. Army ants, for example, do not have a permanent nest. They take their young with them as they move in thousands, consuming every animal that gets in their way. The praying mantis sits still on a plant until an insect comes near. It then shoots out its front pair of legs to catch its prey. There are many kinds of beetle in the rainforest. Some have tails that produce light (without heat) and are known as fireflies. Crickets have a scraper on one wing and a file on the other which they rub together to make a sound. Some invertebrates such as mosquitoes, lice and ticks carry diseases.

THE CONTENTS
Lesson 1 (Ages 5–7)
Rainforest minibeasts

The children colour in and cut out pictures of a range of invertebrates and place them in their classroom rainforest. They learn how to care for a rainforest creature – a stick insect.

Lesson 2 (Ages 7–9)
Fireflies and crickets

The children make a model firefly using a bulb and simple circuit. They communicate by flashing the light in the firefly tails. They also make a file and scraper found on cricket wings to produce a rainforest sound.

Lesson 3 (Ages 9–11)
Rainforest dangers

The children study rainforest invertebrates that carry diseases or poisons and write about encountering them as they make an imaginary journey through the undergrowth.

Notes on photocopiables
Rainforest minibeasts (page 29)

This sheet features life-size pictures for colouring in and cutting out: a praying mantis, leech, beetle, centipede, millipede and a row of army ants.

Fireflies and crickets (page 30)

This photocopiable shows how to make a model firefly with a tail that can light up.

Rainforest dangers (page 31)

This is an information text on invertebrates that carry disease.

IMAGE © HORTONGROU, STOCK.XCHNG

Lesson 1 Rainforest minibeasts

Resources and preparation
- Before the lesson, arrange for the children to go on a minibeast hunt in their local environment to find insects, millipedes, centipedes, woodlice, snails and slugs.
- Each child or small group will need: a photocopy of page 29, coloured pencils, scissors, glue and/or Blu-Tack®.
- For the Extension you will need a plastic tank or large sweet jar with a muslin top. Place in it leafy privet twigs in a small pot of water, and about half a dozen stick insects. You will also need information on stick insect care.

What to do
- Remind the children of their minibeast hunt and talk about the animals they found. They may have seen millipedes, but centipedes are more difficult to see as they soon rush off when they are disturbed.
- Tell the children that some of these kinds of animals are also found in rainforests, but the individuals are a little different.
- Issue the photocopiable sheet and give the children time to realise that the animals are much larger than those in the local environment.
- Ask the children how they can tell a centipede from a millipede, a leech from a beetle and so on. Go on to tell the children that the centipede has a brown body with yellow legs, the millipede is black with grey legs, the ants and leech are brown and the beetle is black.
- Tell the children that after they have coloured and cut out the animals, they can stick them on the walls of their classroom rainforest, among the leaves and tree trunks. Explain that the praying mantis needs to be camouflaged if it is not to be seen by its prey, and ask the children to consider where they will stick the animal (steer them to popping its head over a leaf). They may like to join together to stick all the army ants in one or two parallel lines to show how they march up a tree trunk.

Extension
Tell the children that they can keep insects similar to a praying mantis in the classroom. These creatures are called stick insects and are not predators, but feed on privet. Stick insects live in forests, including rainforests in Asia. The stick insect kept in schools is usually the Indian stick insect, which lives in forests in India. When the stick insects are fully grown they produce eggs (without fertilisation – a zoological oddity!) The eggs can be distinguished from the droppings as they are small shiny barrel shapes with a white cap. If the eggs are placed in a plastic box containing a little leaf mould they may hatch after a few weeks. Let the children learn how to care for them.

AGES 5–7

Objectives
- To compare the local environment with the rainforest environment.
- To learn how to care for a living thing.

Subject references
Science
- Group living things according to observable similarities and differences. (NC: KS1 Sc2 4b)
- Find out about animals in the local environment. (NC: KS1 Sc2 5a)

PSHE and citizenship
- Take and share responsibility (by looking after pets). (NC: KS1 5a)

PHOTOGRAPH © PETER ROWE

Lesson 2 Fireflies and crickets

Objectives
- To investigate how insects communicate.
- To make a model to conduct an investigation.

Subject references
Science
- Learn about the different plants and animals found in different habitats. (NC: KS2 Sc2 5b)
- Construct a circuit incorporating a battery, switch and electrical device. (NC: KS2 Sc4 1a)

Resources and preparation
Each child will need: a strip of corrugated cardboard (ideally single-faced) about 2cm wide and 12cm long, a pen or pencil, photocopiable page 30 copied onto card, scissors, two long wires, a bulb, a battery, a short wire, a switch, sticky tape, paper, Plasticine®; coloured pencils and colour images of fireflies (for more confident learners).

Starter
- Set the scene by telling the children that when someone enters a rainforest they are likely to hear insects communicating with each other. One group of such rainforest insects is the crickets. Each cricket has a scraper on one wing and a file on the other wing, and when it rubs them together it makes a noise that others of its species can recognise. There are many different kinds of cricket and the members of each type can recognise each other by the specific noises they make. Tell the children that they are going to be crickets!
- Hand out the strips of cardboard and demonstrate to the children how to hold the strip in one hand, with the corrugations uppermost, and run the blunt end of a pen or pencil along the grooves to make a sound. Challenge pairs of children to work out a series of rubs to communicate with each other, then let all the 'crickets' communicate at once to reproduce a rainforest sound. The children should also realise that the crickets must have a superior sense of hearing to detect and distinguish sounds from members of their own kind.

What to do
- Tell the children that at night in the rainforest another group of insects called fireflies communicates with each other by flashing light from their tails.
- Remind the children that we normally associate light energy with a release of heat energy, but with fireflies this does not happen. Ask the children what might happen if it did. Look for an answer about the insects roasting themselves!
- Tell the children that they are going to make a model firefly perched on a twig and that they should be able to make its tail flash by operating a switch in a circuit.
- Issue the photocopies of page 30 and go through the process with the children as follows.
– Cut out picture 1, the central rectangle and slits A to B and C to D. Fold the card along the dotted lines so that it can stand up as in picture 3. Stick the bottom tabs to the side tabs to hold this in place. You may

PHOTOGRAPH © PETER ROWE

need to put a lump of Plasticine® in the base to ensure that the stand does not fall over.
– Cut out picture 2 and make the three holes. (You or teaching assistants may need to make the holes for the children.) Push the bulb holder through the holes. Fold tabs E and F and stick them to the back of the card as picture 4 shows. Fix a piece of sticky tape to the bulb holder and attach it to the card at G in picture 4 to hold the bulb holder horizontal.
– Then place the bulb in the holder to build the circuit. Complete the circuit to test that the bulb lights.
– Make and cut out a firefly shape on paper. Stick it to the front of the circuit as picture 3 shows. The bulb should show at the tip of the firefly's tail when the model is viewed from the front.
● Now let pairs of children work out a code of flashes between them. Explain that each pair represents a different kind of firefly and that they can vary the number of flashes given together, the time between each flash or the length of each flash.
● When the children have worked out their codes, let them move to opposite ends of the room with their fireflies, darken the room and let the fireflies flash at each other. Can the children easily recognise a member of their own species and work out the 'message' being sent?

Differentiation
● Help less confident learners in working out a pattern for scraping the cardboard or flashing the light. They may also need help in assembling the circuit model of the firefly on the twig.
● Let more confident learners look at pictures of fireflies and colour in the back of their models and add legs and antennae.

Assessment
The children can be assessed on the success and effect of their firefly circuit constructions.

Plenary
● The children may ask why the insects need to communicate. Explain that the signals are given to bring members of the same type together so that they can breed.
● If some children have made their fireflies more realistic they could be displayed for everyone to examine.

Outcomes
● The children can construct and use a simple circuit for signalling.
● The children understand how some insects use sound and light to communicate.

Did you know?
The glow-worm is a beetle, related to fireflies, that lives in Britain. Its tail makes a steady yellowish light on summer nights.

Lesson 3 Rainforest dangers

IMAGE © PAVOLNAVOL, STOCK.XCHNG; POLAROID IMAGE © KSTYLE, STOCK.XCHNG

AGES 9–11

Objectives
• To become aware of the threat to health caused by some rainforest invertebrates.
• To be able to write creatively about an imaginary expedition through the rainforest.

Subject references
Science
• Learn about different animals in different habitats.
(NC: KS2 Sc2 5b)
• Understand that micro-organisms may be harmful.
(NC: KS2 Sc2 5f)
English
• Plan – note and develop initial ideas.
(NC: KS2 En3 2a)
• Draft – develop ideas from the plan into structured written text.
(NC: KS2 En3 2b)
• Imagine and explore feelings and ideas, focusing on creative use of language and how to interest the reader.
(NC: KS2 En3 9a)

Resources and preparation
Each child will need a photocopy of page 31, paper and pens.

What to do
• Ask the children what they would consider to be dangers in the rainforest. They may mention snakes and large predators such as jaguars. Explain that, in fact, many snakes and large animals move away when they detect people approaching, but nonetheless can be a danger if suddenly surprised or provoked.
• Some children may suggest tarantulas, and use this as a springboard to tell the children that the main and constant dangers to humans in the rainforest do come from smaller animals – invertebrates. Hand out the photocopies of page 31.
• Go through the information on the sheet with the children, then ask them to imagine making a journey through the rainforest and possibly encountering these creatures. Tell the children that it is assumed that they will have taken all the recommended precautions, such as vaccinations and courses of anti-malaria tablets, and are dressed appropriately with only a small amount of skin exposed. Work together with the children to recall what they have already learned about rainforests, such as: the heights of the trees; the density of the canopy and some of the undergrowth; the hot, wet climate; and where some rainforests can be found.
• Let the children plan and discuss some ideas in groups and/or as a whole class before they begin planning and writing their stories individually and in detail.

Extension
The children could use secondary sources to find out more about one of the animals featured on the photocopiable sheet. Challenge them to write a story in which the creature encounters a human in a rainforest, written from the animal's point of view.

Theme 3 **Rainforest minibeasts**

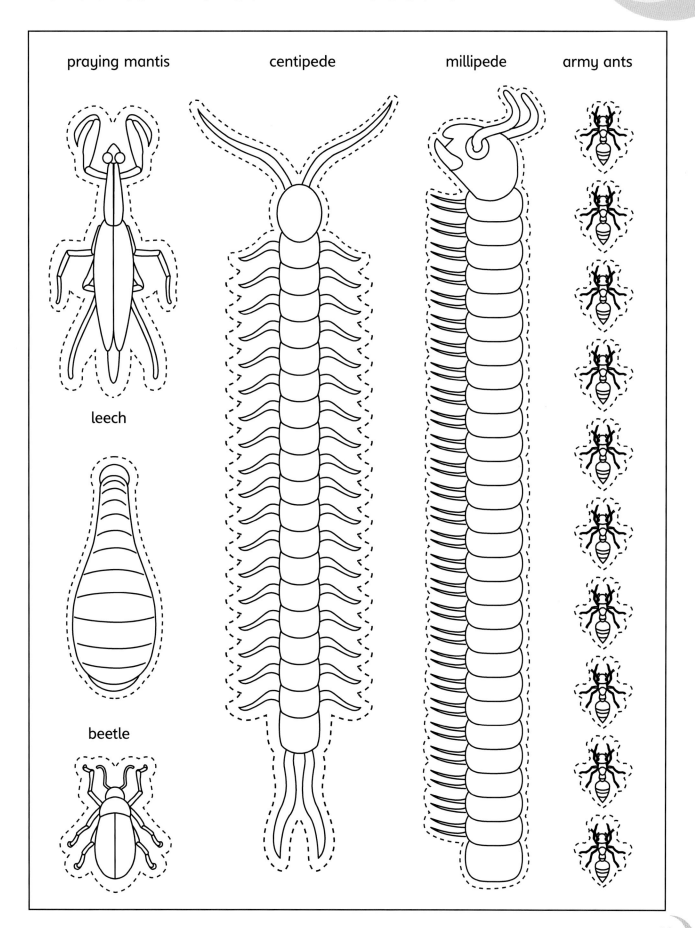

praying mantis   centipede   millipede   army ants

leech

beetle

SCHOLASTIC
www.scholastic.co.uk

Theme 3 Fireflies and crickets

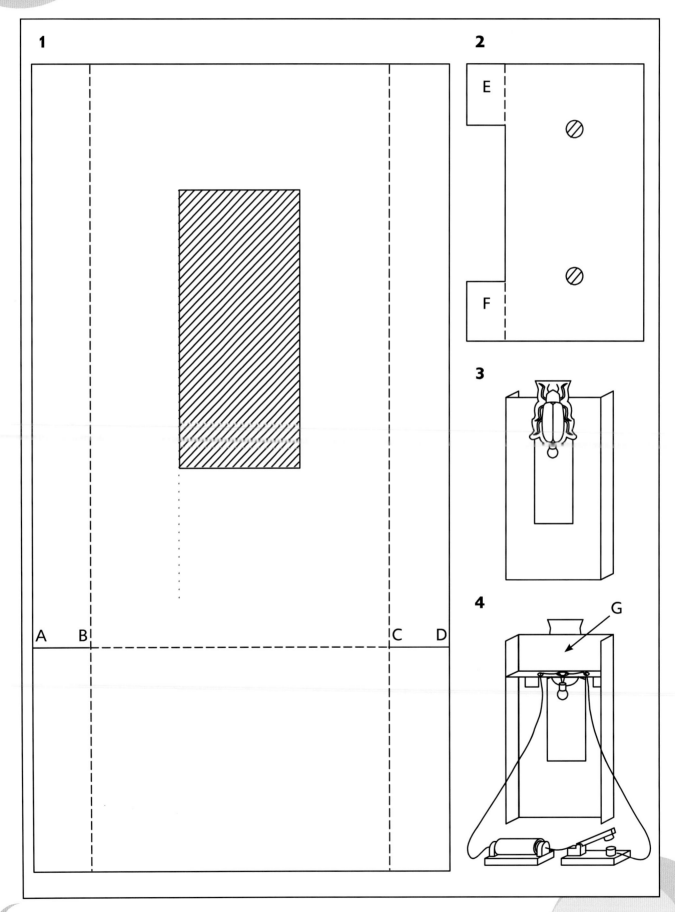

Theme 3 Rainforest dangers

If you went on an expedition in a rainforest, here are some of the animals you could meet that might cause you harm.

Mosquitoes

Some mosquitoes inject their needle-shaped mouths into the skin and suck up your blood. When they do, they might inject you with malaria.

Ticks

A tick uses its eight legs to cling closely to the skin. It bites you then sucks up blood, swells up and falls off. Its saliva can carry germs. The wound it leaves behind can be infected by other rainforest germs.

Leeches

A leech sticks to your skin with its suckers then bites and sucks out some of your blood. As it does so, it swells up. When the leech leaves your skin, the wound it has made can be infected with other germs from the rainforest.

Bees

Bees can become angry if you go too near their nests and swarm after you to attack you with their stings.

Lice

Lice crawl around on your skin and bite into it to draw blood. Their droppings contain typhus germs, which can enter your blood when you scratch your skin.

Ants

Army ants march in huge numbers across the forest floor and bite anything they find to eat – including you!

Spiders

Many spiders are not poisonous, but if you meet a dark-coloured spider with spots of red, yellow or white – beware! The funnel web spider of Australia is grey or brown and deadly poisonous too.

Rainforest vertebrates

BACKGROUND

Vertebrates are animals that have a skeleton of bone. The five major divisions of the vertebrate group are fish, amphibians, reptiles, birds and mammals. A rainforest has many streams and rivers, populated with fish such as piranha and the neon tetra fish. The rainforest is home to many kinds of amphibian and reptile: frogs, snakes and lizards live in the trees, while turtles, crocodiles and alligators live in the rivers. Birds and mammals are found at all levels in the rainforest. There are only a few kinds of large mammal that live on the forest floor, such as the tapir and the peccary. Jaguars and leopards visit the lower branches, while monkeys live in the canopy. Bats fly through the spaces in the understorey and undergrowth. Monkeys are found in rainforests across the world. Biologists split the world into two when considering monkey species: the New World (North and South America) and the Old World (Africa and south-east Asia). Many New World monkeys have prehensile tails, which can be used as a fifth limb. Old World monkeys do not have prehensile tails. Apes do not have tails.

THE CONTENTS
Lesson 1 (Ages 5–7)
Move like an animal
The children learn and copy the movements of different vertebrates.

Lesson 2 (Ages 7–9)
Monkeys and apes
The children identify different monkeys and apes and locate their habitats. They use secondary sources to profile a monkey or ape of their choice.

Lesson 3 (Ages 9–11)
A rainforest food web
The children construct food chains and link them together to form a food web.

Notes on photocopiables
Move like an animal (page 37)
This page shows a range of animals and how they move.

Monkeys and apes (page 38)
This page features 14 different monkeys and apes. There are visual clues on how to tell an ape from a monkey and how to tell an Old World monkey from a New World monkey. New World Monkeys with prehensile tails are: woolly monkey, squirrel monkey, spider monkey, howler monkey, capuchin monkey (all South American). Monkeys without prehensile tails are: (in Africa) mandrill, colobus, mangabey; (in south-east Asia) proboscis and macaque. Apes are: (in Africa) chimpanzee and gorilla; (in south-east Asia) gibbon and orang-utan.

A rainforest food web (page 39)
This is a food web of the Amazonian rainforest. The food chains are: Roots–agouti–anaconda; Roots–agouti–jaguar; Roots–peccary–anaconda; Roots-peccary-jaguar; Leaves–tapir–jaguar; Leaves–sloth–jaguar; Leaves–capuchin monkey–jaguar; Flowers–butterflies–capuchin–jaguar; Flowers–butterflies–capuchin–harpy eagle; Fruit–spider monkey–harpy eagle; Fruit–macaw–harpy eagle. The herbivores are: agouti, peccary, tapir, sloth, butterfly, capuchin monkey (in leaves chain), spider monkey, macaw. The carnivores are: anaconda, jaguar, harpy eagle and capuchin monkey (in flowers chain). Animals that feed on plants *and* animals, like the capuchin monkey, are omnivores.

IMAGE © GRAFINET, STOCK.XCHNG

Lesson 1 Move like an animal

IMAGE © GASTONMAG, STOCK.XCHNG

POLAROID IMAGES: TOP © PROTOTYPE7, STOCK.XCHNG; BOTTOM © KIT1578, STOCK.XCHNG

AGES 5–7

Objectives
● To learn how different kinds of animal move.
● To mime the different kinds of animal movement.

Subject references
English
● Use actions to convey characters.
(NC: KS1 En1 4a)
● Work in role.
(NC: KS1 En1 11a)
Physical education
● Explore basic skills.
(NC: KS1 1a)
● Remember and repeat simple actions with increasing control and coordination.
(NC: KS1 1b)

Resources and preparation
● Each group will need a photocopy of page 37.
● You will also need: pictures of a (rainforest) snake, frog, bat, jaguar, tapir, sloth, harpy eagle and marmoset, a large space (such as the school hall), a globe (optional).

What to do
● Show the children the pictures of the various rainforest animals. Encourage them to learn the names and be able to recognise them. Examine their different features, such as limbs, wings and tails.
● Tell the children that all the animals live in the rainforest in South America and show them the position of the rainforest on a globe.
● Hand out the photocopies of page 37. Encourage the children to recognise the animals from the pictures they have just looked at. Read and discuss each kind of movement in turn. Demonstrate how the body can be made to mime the movement. For example, when a tapir walks quickly, it picks its feet straight up and then puts them straight down. The movement of the sloth can be made by lying on the floor with arms and legs slowly creeping along in the

air. The marmoset runs along branches and hops to the next one. It has quick and jerky movements.
● Let the children try to mime the movements. You could call out the name of an animal and see if the children can remember how it moves, or you can tell them to slither like a snake! and so on.

Extension
Ask the children to work together to perform a mime of jungle life. Eight children could be the different animals and work in the following pairs:
● A snake could slither after a frog, which hops away in the nick of time.
● A jaguar could prowl around and stalk a tapir, then the tapir trots off before the jaguar can pounce.
● A sloth can look around and move along slowly as a bat flies by.
● A harpy eagle can soar around and swoop down after a marmoset, which hops and runs away.
● Several children could be frogs, tapirs, bats and marmosets in the mime.
This activity could be developed as a mime to accompany the song in Theme 9.

TOPICS Rainforests

Lesson 2 Monkeys and apes

AGES 7–9

Objectives
● To know the location of the more well-known monkeys and apes.
● To distinguish between apes and monkeys.
● To construct a profile of an ape or a monkey.

Subject references
Science
● Learn that the variety of different animals makes it important to identify them and assign them to groups. (NC: KS2 Sc2 4c)
Geography
● Know the location of environments they study. (NC: KS2 3b)
ICT
● Talk about what information they need and how they can find and use it. (NC: KS2 1a)
● Prepare information for development. (NC: KS2 1b)
● Develop and refine ideas by bringing together, organising and reorganising, text, and images. (NC: KS2 2a)

Resources and preparation
Each child or small group will need: photocopiable page 15 mounted in the centre of A3 paper or card, photocopies of page 38, pens or pencils, scissors, glue. They will also need access to information about apes and monkeys from books, CD-ROMs and websites, as well as computer access and appropriate software to prepare their profiles.

Starter
Ask the children if they have been to a zoo and, if so, what animals they saw and which was their favourite. Listen out for mentions of monkeys and apes and steer the conversation around to them being popular animals in zoos and on wildlife television programmes. Ask the children if they can name some kinds of monkey and say where they come from. Then ask if they know where apes such as chimpanzees or gibbons come from. There may be confusion or blank looks in response to some of these questions, so tell the children that they are going to find out more!

What to do
● Issue the maps from photocopiable page 15 and show the children where to put labels for South America, Africa and South-east Asia.
● Now hand out the photocopies of page 38 and let the children cut out the animals after they have read the captions. Help them to arrange the pictures near the area where the animals are found and glue them in place around the edge of the map. Ask them to draw label lines from each animal picture to the approximate centre of its rainforest region. You will need to clarify that this labelling simply shows the regions where the animals live, but does not indicate that they all live in the same part of the rainforest.
● Move on to tell the children that some monkeys have prehensile tails. This means that they can use their tail a little bit like a hand: they curl the tip of the tail around a branch, for example, and use it for support as a fifth limb. Ask the children to write a list of the monkeys with this feature (shown in the illustrations with a curl in the tail) and state in which rainforest they are found. Then ask them to list monkeys which do not have prehensile tails and to state the rainforests in which they are found.
● Now talk about apes, and tell the children that apes do not have tails. Ask them to write down a list of apes and the

Did you know?

Chimpanzees use sticks to poke ants' nests and collect insects. They lick off the ants that climb onto the stick.

rainforests in which they are found.

• Finally, let the children browse their maps to select a monkey or an ape and find out as much about it as they can. Give them time to prepare a profile of the animal using ICT, which should include labelled pictures and information on where it comes from and the kind of tail it has.

Differentiation

• Help less confident learners to locate the forests in which the apes and monkeys live. They may need guidance on how to find information on the monkey or ape they have chosen.

• Tell more confident learners that monkeys and apes belong to a larger group of mammals called primates. Also in this group are animals such as bushbabies, lorises, pottos and marmosets. Encourage children to research these animals and select one to profile, perhaps noting any

differences between this animal and the ape or monkey they profiled earlier.

Assessment

The children can be assessed on the accuracy of their answers to the work with the photocopiable sheets and on the quality of their profiles.

Plenary

Let the children display their profiles on or near the classroom rainforest wall or give a presentation on what they have discovered. Use the maps to confirm the differences between Old World and New World monkeys.

Outcomes

• The children realise that apes, monkeys and other primates are inhabitants of the rainforest.

• The children learn to distinguish between monkeys and apes and between New World and Old World monkeys.

Lesson 3 A rainforest food web

Objectives
● To learn how the lives of rainforest animals are related to each other through feeding.
● To realise that if one forest organism is removed the lives of the others can be affected.

Subject references
Science
● Use food chains to show feeding relationships in a habitat.
(NC: KS2 Sc2 5a)
● Know that nearly all food chains start with a green plant.
(NC: KS2 Sc2 5b)

Resources and preparation
● Each child or small group will need: a photocopy of page 39, paper, pens.
● You will need: pictures of a peccary, jaguar, spider monkey and harpy eagle and of the other animals featured on page 39.

What to do
● Tell the children that in the Amazonian rainforest there is a pig-like animal called a peccary that feeds on plant roots. Show them its picture. If they do not already know about it, tell them that this rainforest is also home to a large member of the cat family called the jaguar, which preys on the peccary. Show them its picture too.
● Ask for a volunteer to come to the board and draw a food chain linking the roots and the animals (roots → peccary → jaguar).
● Tell the children that up in the forest canopy spider monkeys feed on fruit. Show them its picture. Tell them that the harpy eagle flies above the canopy and dives into it to catch spider monkeys. Show a picture of the eagle.
● Ask another volunteer to come to the board and draw a food chain linking the fruit and the animals (fruit → spider monkey → harpy eagle).
● Now ask the children to help you construct a fuller food chain from the following information: capuchin monkeys feed on butterflies, butterflies feed on flowers, jaguars feed on capuchin monkeys. (flowers → butterflies → capuchin monkey → jaguar). Write the chain on the board.
● Point out that the first and third food chains end in the same animal (jaguar) and therefore can be joined at the jaguar. Say that most animals eat a variety of foods and can be linked into a food web by their feeding habits.
● Issue the photocopies of page 39 and display pictures of the animals included. Ask the children to identify and write out the different food chains. Can the children identify the herbivore and carnivore in each chain?

Extension
Ask the children how the animals in the forest would be affected if there were no longer a) flowers (butterflies move away, capuchin monkeys eat more leaves and fruit), b) fruit (spider monkey and macaw move away, harpy eagles eat more capuchin monkeys, more butterflies survive, jaguars eat more of other prey), c) leaves (tapir and sloth move away; capuchin monkeys eat more butterflies; agoutis eat more roots; jaguars eat more agoutis, peccaries and capuchin monkeys; anaconda has less food). There are more consequences to be considered further around the food web. Finally, ask what would happen if the roots, leaves, flowers and fruit were all removed. (All the animals would die, as not only their food has gone but also their habitat.)

IMAGES FROM LEFT TO RIGHT: © DBGEORGE, STOCK.XCHNG; © POOKIEPIX, STOCK.XCHNG; © COREL DISCS; © RIAHNMAN, STOCK.XCHNG; © ZEAFONSO, STOCK.XCHNG

HOT**TOPICS** Rainforests

Theme 4 Move like an animal

Flap like a bat

Soar like an eagle

Hop and run like a marmoset

Rest like a sloth

Slither like a snake

Trot like a tapir

Prowl like a jaguar

Hop like a frog

Theme 4 Monkeys and apes

chimpanzee Africa	woolly monkey South America
mandrill Africa	gibbon south-east Asia
squirrel monkey South America	proboscis monkey south-east Asia
gorilla Africa	colobus monkey Africa
spider monkey South America	orang-utan south-east Asia
mangabey Africa	howler monkey South America
capuchin monkey South America	macaque south-east Asia

Theme 4 A rainforest food web

A food web in the rainforest

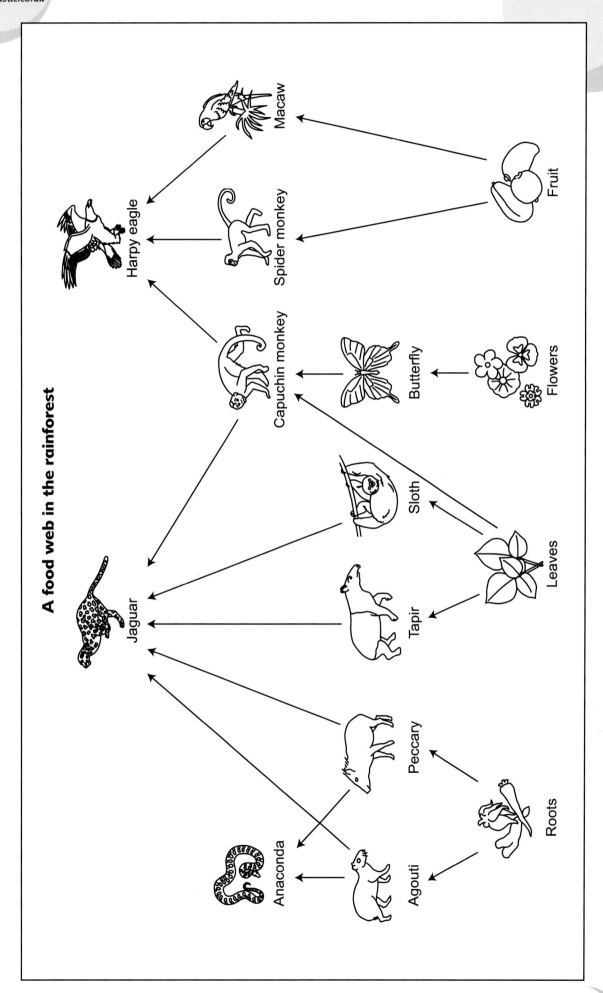

Rainforest people

BACKGROUND

The Yanomami tribe of the South American rainforest make large communal buildings called *yanos*. Each family makes its section and these are joined to make one structure. In the children's model the roof is flat, for simplicity, but a real yano has a sloping roof to allow rainwater to run off. There are no walls between each section of the yano and each family sleeps in a hammock. The central area is used for celebration dances. Millions of people used to live in the rainforests. It is thought that about six million people lived in the Amazonian rainforest before the Europeans arrived, but today the number is probably less than a quarter of a million.

The Aztecs can be traced back to north Mexico in about AD 1100. After setting up the city Tenochtitlan, they eventually took over the whole of the Valley of Mexico. In 1440, Moctezuma I became ruler and their empire expanded until 1502. The Spanish arrived on the Mexican coast in 1519 and by 1521 they had defeated the Aztecs.

THE CONTENTS
Lesson 1 (Ages 5–7)
Make a yano
Each group makes a section of a model yano, then six groups join to make one yano.

Lesson 2 (Ages 7–9)
The Aztecs
The children learn about the Aztec empire and add it to a timeline. They make a 20-day calendar, a farmhouse and *chinampa*.

Lesson 3 (Ages 9–11)
Living in the rainforest
The children learn how rainforest people gather food and use materials sustainably.

Notes on photocopiables
Make a yano (page 45)
This is a template for making a model yano. The illustrations show how a section looks when it is constructed and how a model with six sections looks when seen from above.

The Aztecs (page 46)
The symbols on the border of this page are for the 20-day calendar for the children to cut out. Anticlockwise from top left, they are: crocodile, wind, house, lizard, serpent, death, deer, rabbit, water, dog, monkey, grass, reed, jaguar, eagle, vulture, motion, knife, rain, flower. There are also diagrams showing how to make a model farmhouse and chinampa.

Rainforest people (page 47)
This report tells of how a tribe sets up home in the rainforest and lives there without causing permanent damage.
Answers: 1) It lets in light that the plants need to grow; 2) It destroys leaves and branches so light can reach the soil and it provides minerals for plant growth; 3) Insects could gather easily, breed and feed on the plants so the tribe would have nothing to eat; 4) Sometimes there would not be too much food and sometimes there wouldn't be enough and the tribe would have to spend more time hunting and gathering; 5) Very important. They are used for food, making homes, hammocks and poisons for hunting; 6) From the plants that they cut down to make the clearing; 7) The animals might only be wounded and could move away. It would be hard for the hunters to follow them through the undergrowth to shoot them again; 8) They do not destroy their environment, but care for it; they only use what they need.

IMAGE © MIKEKWIK, STOCK.XCHNG

HOTTOPICS Rainforests

Lesson 1 Make a yano

Resources and preparation

- Each child or small group will need: a photocopy of page 45, coloured pencils, scissors, sticky tape. For the Extension, they will need pencils and paper.
- You will also need pictures of the Yanomami tribe in their homes.

What to do

- Tell the children that people in the rainforest live in groups called tribes. Each tribe is made up of many families and each family makes a home, which is attached to its neighbours so that they all live in a large circular building called a yano. Show the diagram on the photocopiable sheet and point out the space in the middle for dances and communal celebrations.
- Hand out the sheet and tell the children that they are going to make a model of one family home and join it to five others to make a yano. Point out the roof and say that it is made from palm leaves. Ask the children to draw interlocking leaves on the roof template. Next, say that the wall is made with thick vertical sticks. Ask the children to draw these in.
- Direct the children to look at the roof supports and how they are positioned. They are made of strong pieces of wood and should be coloured brown.
- Let the children cut out the pieces and join them with sticky tape. They will need to connect the top of the wall to the roof using tabs X, Y and Z. They will need to fold the supports lengthways, cut between tabs A and B, and C and D, bend the tabs at right angles and stick them to the underside of the roof with sticky tape.
- When six children or groups have made their homes, let them join them together as shown. There will probably be variation in the quality of the buildings, but real yanos also show variation in building, and may form ovals, so it is not important to have a perfect circle.
- In a real yano, there would be a gap for an entrance. See if the children can work out which home should be made a little smaller in order to cut in a gap.

Extension

Show the pictures of the yano to the children and talk about; the absence of walls, sleeping in hammocks, cooking on fires and keeping pets such as dogs, monkeys or parrots. Challenge the children to invent a story about life as a member of the tribe.

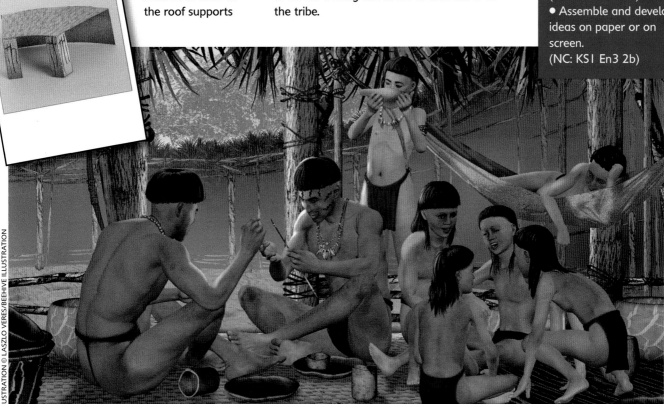

AGES 5–7

Objectives
- To learn about the home of a rainforest people.
- To make a model of the home.
- To work with others to assemble a communal building.

Subject references
Design and technology
- Select tools, techniques and materials for making their product. (NC: KS1 2a)
- Assemble, join and combine components, identify what they could have done differently and how they could improve on their work in the future. (NC: KS1 2d)

English
- Tell imagined stories. (NC: KS1 En1 8a)
- Assemble and develop ideas on paper or on screen. (NC: KS1 En3 2b)

Lesson 2 The Aztecs

AGES 7–9

Objectives
- To understand that the Aztecs had a different way of measuring time.
- To make a model Aztec house.
- To learn how the Aztecs produced enough food for their huge population.

Subject references
History
- Place people in correct periods of time. (NC: KS2 1a)
- Identify characteristic features of a society. (NC: KS2 2a)
- Study a society in relation to other societies, houses and cities. (NC: KS2 13)

Design and technology
- Generate ideas for products. (NC: KS2 1a)
- Measure mark out, cut a range of materials and assemble and combine components and materials accurately. (NC: KS2 2d)

Mathematics
- Choose and use suitable measuring instruments for a task. (NC: KS2 Ma3 4b)

Resources and preparation
- For the starter, you will need the following dates on a set of large cards (or you could use an interactive whiteboard and have the information in separate boxes that can be moved around the screen): The Aztecs 1195–1521; The Egyptians 3100bc–ad30; The Ancient Greeks 900bc–148bc; The Romans 735bc–ad476; The Anglo Saxons 350–1066; The Vikings 793–1035; The Tudors 1485–1603; The Victorians 1831–1901.
- Each child or group will need: photocopiable page 46 copied onto card, scissors, a paper clip, card.
- If children will make a calendar holder, provide pieces of card, glue, some pictures showing Aztec life, which could help to stimulate design ideas.
- More confident children will need metre rules or a tape measure and canes for measuring out a chinampa.

Starter
- Tell the children that a group of people who lived in Mexico settled in the Valley of Mexico in around 1195. In 1325, at Lake Texcoco they built a city called Tenochtitlan on an island. In time, the population spread out, conquered the lands around them and built up a large empire. In 1521, Spaniards arrived and put Tenochtitlan under siege. The Aztecs eventually surrendered and their empire was lost.
- Set up the date cards at the front of the classroom in random order and ask the children to help you to arrange them in chronological order so that you can make a timeline to show how the Aztecs fitted in with other periods and peoples of history.

What to do
- Tell the children that the Aztecs had a complicated calendar, within which each month had 20 days. Issue the photocopies of page 46 and explain that the Aztecs invented a kind of picture writing: the days of the month are shown in the border. Ask the children to guess what the symbols represent. (The month starts with the day of the crocodile and you follow the pictures in an anticlockwise direction to come to the last day of the month – the day of the flower).
- Let the children cut out the pictures, arrange them in order from front to back and hold them together with a paper clip. Alternatively, you may like them to design and make a holder for the cards.
- Move on to tell the children that as the Aztec city of Tenochtitlan increased in size, more land was needed to grow food for the increasing population. The Aztecs solved the problem by building chinampas. Mud was dug up from the lake and piled up to make an island between 6m and 10m wide and

PHOTOGRAPH © PETER ROWE

between 30m and 61m long. The mud was held in place by walls made of branches woven together, and willow trees were planted so that their roots could hold the soil in place. Crops such as maize, beans, squashes and peppers were grown.

• On a larger chinampa, a farmer could erect a house for himself and his family. The house would have one or two rooms. Ask the children to cut the model house from the photocopiable sheet and assemble it. Tell them to fold along all the lines and use the tabs to stick the ends of the houses to the roof and long sides.

• Look at the illustration of the chinampa with its house and give the children some card to make a chimpana for their house.

Differentiation

• Less confident learners may need help in thinking of a design for a calendar holder. You may also want to enlarge the templates for the house to ease cutting and assembly.

• More confident learners could measure out and mark the sizes of two chinampas (one that is 6m by 30m and one 10m by 60m) on the school field for the whole class to look at.

Assessment

The children can be assessed on the design of their calendar holders and the construction of their houses and chinampas.

Plenary

• Let the children gather their chinampa together as a village. Tell them that the Aztecs built canals between the chinampas, wide enough to allow two canoes to pass each other. Arrange the chinampa accordingly.

• The children might want to keep their calendars on their desks and turn them every day. If you plan a Rainforest Day in the next three weeks, the children can work out what day it will be on their calendar and count down to the day in Aztec days.

Outcomes

• The children can make a calendar holder and use the Aztec calendar.

• The children can make a model farmhouse and chinampa.

Lesson 3 Living in the rainforest

IMAGE © TIBO, _TOC <.XCHNG; POLAROID IMAGE © HDE2003. STOCK.XCHNG.

AGES 9–11

Objectives
- To learn how people live in rainforests without harming their environment.
- To know where people can be found living in rainforests today.

Subject references
English
- Use inference and deduction.
(NC: KS2 En2 2a)
- Make connections between different parts of the text.
(NC: KS2 En2 2c)
- Obtain specific information through detailed reading.
(NC: KS2 En2 3c)
Geography
- Use atlases and maps.
(NC: KS2 2c)
- Study a range of places and environments in different parts of the world.
(NC: KS2 7b)

Did you know?
In the past, some rainforest tribes believed that shrinking the heads of their enemies gave them power.

Resources and preparation
- Each child will need a photocopy of page 47, paper and pens; (for the Extension) their photocopies of page 15, atlases.
- You will need pictures of rainforest people tending their crops and hunting.

What to do
- Show the children some pictures of rainforest people going about their everyday tasks, and ask the children what they can deduce about their way of life. Talk, for example, about what seems to be their independent, self-sufficient life, in terms of growing their own crops, hunting their own food and building their own homes.
- Issue the photocopies of page 47 and let the children read the text and answer the questions about it.
- Then go through the answers with the children. Stress the ways in which the rainforest people live in harmony with their environment and how their approach to life maintains the balance of the environment so preserving it for future generations.
- Compare this respectful approach with that of some people and governments in other parts of the world.
- Ask the children for their views on the future of the rainforest, a topic which you can return to in later themes.

Extension
- Tell the children that the people who live in each rainforest region are divided into many tribes. They share the same basic approach to life in the rainforest as outlined on page 47 but have differences in, for example, the way they dress, decorate their bodies and build their homes. Write down the names of the following tribes on the board together with the rainforest region where they live:
– Yanomami, Wai Wai and Kayap'o live in the Amazonian rainforest.
– Baka, Bayaka and Efe live in the African rainforest. (These tribes are members of a larger group known widely as Pygmies).
– Penan live in the Rainforests of Borneo (specifically, Sarawak).
– Huli and Medi in the rainforests of New Guinea.
– Djabuganjdiji live in the rainforests of Queensland, Australia. (They are Aboriginal Australians.)
- Give out the children's copies of the map on page 15 along with atlases and let the children add to their maps with labels of the places where each tribe lives.

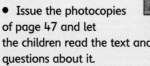

PHOTOCOPIABLE

Theme 5 Make a yano

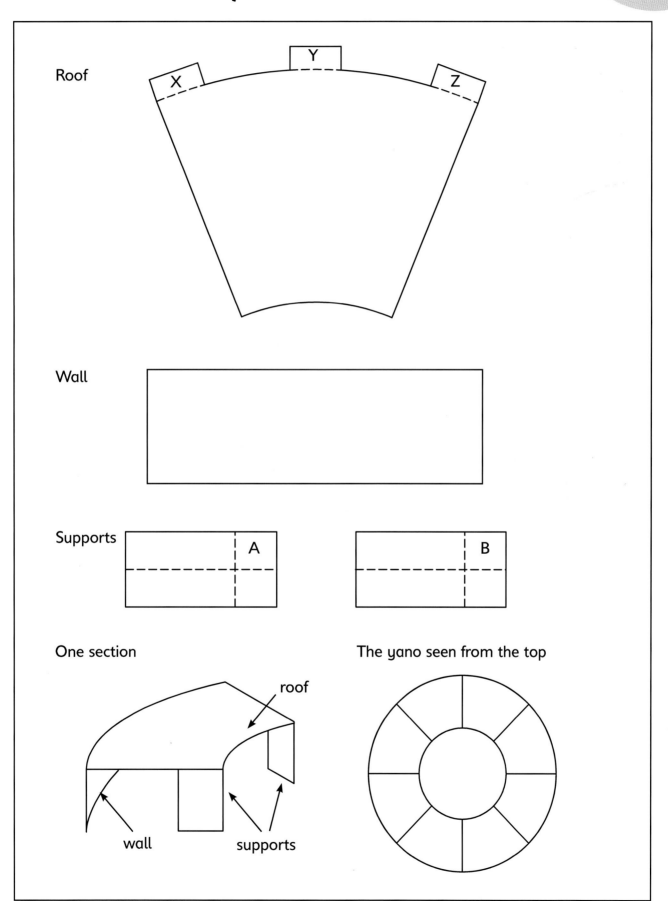

Roof

Wall

Supports

One section

The yano seen from the top

■ SCHOLASTIC
www.scholastic.co.uk

Theme 5 The Aztecs

HOT TOPICS Rainforests

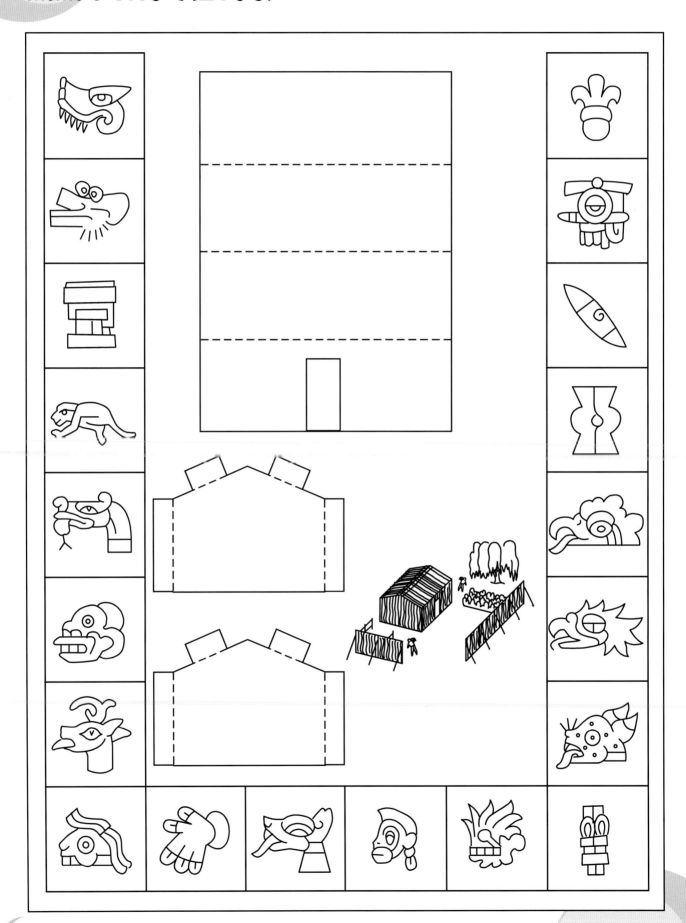

Theme 5 Living in the rainforest

A tree falls. It makes a small clearing in the rainforest. Some time later, a group of tribesmen walk into the clearing and decide it is a place they could make their new home.

They cut down more trees and undergrowth to make the clearing larger. They burn some of the wood and leaves to make ash. The ash mixes with the forest soil and provides minerals for the crops the tribe will grow. Plants such as yams, plantains, maize and manioc are grown together in the forest garden. The plants are mixed up rather than grown in separate patches. This prevents large numbers of insects breeding and feeding on their favourite plants. The crops are planted in stages so that they can be harvested at different times of year and provide a constant food supply.

The families build their homes in the clearing. They use branches to make the framework, and vines to tie it together and to attach the palm leaves used for the roof. Cord made from strong plant fibres is used to make hammocks, which hang inside the homes.

People wear down tracks around the settlement so they can move around easily to gather fruits and nuts. Some plants and animals provide poisons which the hunters use on their darts and arrows. The poison makes the hunted animal fall immediately and prevents a wounded animal being chased through the forest. The hunters use bows and arrows for animals close to the forest floor, and blowpipes and darts for animals such as parrots and monkeys which live higher in the forest vegetation. Any poison in the meat is destroyed in cooking.

After two or three years, the minerals in the soil are used up and crops begin to fail. Then the tribesmen look for a new place to set up home, and the tribe moves away. Seeds that fall from the plants around the clearing soon germinate. The seedlings then grow quickly and the area is filled with forest plants once again. All trace of the tribe eventually disappears. Many years later, another tree here may fall and make another small clearing. It may be visited by the great grandchildren of the tribe and become their home for a while.

1. How does making a clearing help the tribe to grow crops?

2. Name two ways in which burning the undergrowth is useful.

3. What would happen if the crops were planted in separate patches?

4. What would happen if all the crops were ready at the same time?

5. How important are plants in the lives of the people? Explain your answer.

6. Where do you think the tribe gets its materials for making the homes?

7. Why would hunting without poison be more difficult?

8. It has been said that rainforest tribes live in harmony with their environment. What do you think this means?

Disappearing rainforests

BACKGROUND

The reasons for rainforest destruction are many and complex. Briefly, most rainforests are in poor countries often in debt to richer countries through loans that have helped to sustain them. In order to repay the debts, the poor countries have to sell their resources. Rainforest timber provides material for furniture building and for paper. The cleared land is then a place to rear cattle (or crops such as oil palms) to provide meat for the rich countries.

Rainforest plants have extensive root systems that prevent rain from washing the soil and minerals away and quickly take up minerals from decayed leaves and logs. This means that most of the minerals are stored in the plants rather than the soil. When a rainforest is cleared, a mineral-poor soil is exposed for growing crops such as grass, but the rain soon washes the soil away as there are no roots to hold it in place.

Some smaller areas of rainforest have been completely destroyed by open-cast mining, although companies are now supposed to re-establish growth when the mine is no longer of use. Hydroelectric power schemes require dams across rivers, which cause large areas of rainforest to be lost under water.

THE CONTENTS

Lesson 1 (Ages 5–7)
Timber!

The children cut out six pictures showing the destruction of the rainforest and arrange them in the correct order. They discuss what they can see in each picture and their feelings about what the whole sequence shows. They learn how to make some recycled paper.

Lesson 2 (Ages 7–9)
Selling it off

The children develop, rehearse and perform a play from a simple script. The play is intended to generate concern, and it has a slightly downbeat ending. This can be alleviated by following the play with a presentation about alternatives to rainforest exploitation, or the song from Theme 9 Lesson 1.

Lesson 3 (Ages 9–11)
Rainforest destruction

The children research books and the internet to produce a report about rainforest destruction. They look at maps and satellite images and visualise the rate of destruction per second using images of the football grounds of their favourite teams.

Notes on photocopiables
Timber! (page 53)

These six pictures show the stages in the destruction of a rainforest, but they are mixed up. The children cut them out and arrange them in the correct order. The pictures should stimulate discussion. The correct order for the pictures is: top left, bottom right, top right, bottom left, middle right and middle left.

Selling it off (pages 54 and 55)

This playscript introduces government and corporate involvement in the business side of the rainforest. (There are suggestions for performing the play in the What to do section.)

There is no photocopiable for Lesson 3.

IMAGE © EJBEVAN, STOCK.XCHNG

Lesson 1 Timber!

IMAGE © CX. ED. STOCK.XCHNG

AGES 5–7

Objectives
● To learn about one way the rainforests are being destroyed.
● To learn how to make recycled paper.

Subject references
Geography
● Recognise how places are linked to other places in the world.
(NC: KS1 3e)
● Recognise changes in the environment.
(NC: KS1 5a)
History
● Place events in chronological order.
(NC: KS1 1a)
English
● Make relevant comments.
(NC: KS1 En1 2c)
● Write to communicate to others.
(NC: KS1 En3 8a)

Resources and preparation
● Each child or group will need: a photocopy of page 53, scissors, paper, pencils.
● For the Extension, they will need: shredded waste paper, a bowl of water, spoon, metal gauze or grill to support a thin layer of paper pulp, smooth board (such as a large chopping board), rolling pin, felt-tipped pens.

What to do
● Tell the children that large areas of the rainforests are being destroyed very quickly at the moment in order to provide wood for furniture and paper. Give the children some indication of what it would be like by pulling down some the paper tree branches or palms from the classroom rainforest. Be prepared for outrage!
● Issue the photocopies of page 53 and tell the children that it shows the stages in the destruction of a rainforest but the pictures are all mixed up. Ask the children to cut out the pictures and arrange them in the correct order.
● Discuss each picture in turn and ask the children to tell you what they can see.
● When you have established the sequence of events and discussed each picture, encourage the children to talk about what they think about the destruction of the rainforest and what they think could be done to stop the destruction.
● The children could write about rainforests being cut down, using the pictures from the photocopiable to help them structure their writing. They could include some of the points you have discussed as a class, such as the feelings of the people driven out of their homes.

Extension
If the children have not already suggested it, introduce the use of recycled paper as one method of reducing deforestation. Their homes and the school may make use of a council recycling programme. Help the children to make some recycled paper by mixing shredded used paper with water to make a pulp. Then put a thin layer of pulp on a metal gauze or grill. Carefully tip the pulp out of the gauze or grill, on to a board. Press the pulp with a rolling pin before leaving it to dry out completely. The children can then test their paper by writing a slogan on it that they have devised about recycling paper.

Lesson 2 Selling it off

AGES 7–9

Objectives
● To learn about ways in which rainforests are being destroyed.
● To perform a written play or improvise a drama about the destruction of the rainforest.
● To develop teamwork skills.

Subject references
English
● Create, adapt and sustain different roles, individually or in groups.
(NC: KS2 En1 4a)
● Use action and narrative to convey emotions in plays they devise.
(NC: KS2 En1 4b)
Art and design
● Collect visual and other information to help them develop their ideas.
(NC: KS2 1c)
● Combine visual qualities of materials and match them to the purpose of the work.
(NC: KS2 2a)
● Compare approaches in their own and others' work and say what they think and feel about them.
(NC: KS2 3a)

Resources and preparation
● Each child will need photocopies of pages 54 and 55.
● You will need materials and equipment for the following costumes: eight or ten rainforest trees, two rainforest birds, two monkeys, a sloth, eight cows, two rainforest people, two lumberjacks, a farmer, three government officials and two company representatives. You might also want to provide picture references for these figures.
● You will also need materials and equipment for making model chainsaws, plenty of teaching assistants and time for making costumes and holding rehearsals.

Starter
Tell the children about how rainforests are being destroyed to provide timber for furniture and paper and space for rearing beef cattle. Explain to the children that you would like them to perform a play about this situation, and say that you have one that they can use or adapt. Explain that there are at least 28 people in the play, so everyone can have a part.

What to do
● Issue the photocopies of the playscript and show the children that it contains the dialogue for the first three scenes of the play. You could use this opportunity to discuss how they can tell it is a playscript rather than a story book. (The characters' names are listed down the side, it is predominantly speech but there is no use of said... or speech marks, there are instructions, or stage directions, explaining how the actors should move, there are no paragraph descriptions of settings and actions, and so on.)
● Ask the children to listen as you talk them through how the stage is set up and introduce some of the characters.
● Read through the script with the children. Ask them what they thought about the destruction of the rainforests before reading it, and how they think the play is supposed to make them feel. How do they feel?
● Describe the resources you have available and then discuss with the children how the costumes should be made. Organise sessions for designing and making

the costumes and props. Encourage the children to help each other with ideas and techniques and discuss progress. Let the children look at references if they want their costumes and props to look fairly authentic.

• Cast the actors and read through the play several times. Let the children change or add extra pieces to it if they wish. You may want to divide the class into groups by scene to allow them to rehearse and develop their scripts in more detail.

Differentiation

• Less confident learners may need help making the costumes and following stage directions. Children who are less confident speaking in front of an audience may prefer to take the parts of one of the cows, or a tree.

• More confident learners may like to add more dialogue and action. If you divide the class into groups, one child per group could also act as director, making sure that the

stage directions are followed. The more demanding roles in the play are those of the meat dealer, farmer and government official.

Assessment

The children could be assessed on the quality of the costumes they make, their contribution to the development of the play and their performance.

Plenary

After sufficient rehearsal, the play can be performed, in full costume, to the whole school as part of Rainforest Day. It could also be performed to parents and carers on another occasion.

Outcomes

• The children learn about ways in which rainforests are destroyed.

• The children take part in a play.

ILLUSTRATION © LASZLO VERES/BEEHIVE ILLUSTRATION

Lesson 3 Rainforest destruction

Objectives
- To learn about the destruction of the rainforest.
- To compile a report on a topical issue using material from various sources.

Subject references
Geography
- Recognise some human processes and explain how these can cause changes in environments.
(NC: KS2 4b)
- Explore an environmental issue.
(NC: KS2 6e)

English
- Obtain specific information through detailed reading.
(NC: KS2 En2 3c)
- Develop ideas from a plan into structured written text.
(NC: KS2 En3 2b)

ICT
- Prepare information for development using ICT.
(NC: KS2 1a)
- Work with a range of information to consider its characteristics and purposes.
(NC: KS2 5a)

Resources and preparation
- You will need a selection of books and news articles on the rainforest along with internet access, paper and pencils or presentation software. (A list of useful websites is provided here, but you will need to check that they are still active before the lesson.) The site www.rain-tree.com/facts.htm contains a great deal of information. Direct the children to scroll down to the sections: The disappearing rainforests, The importance of the rainforest and The driving forces of destruction. The site www.rainforestfoundationuk.org/s-news contains up-to-date news, but is really for adults. You may like to browse through it and select some items to discuss with the class.
- For the Extension, the children will need access to http://maps.google.com, tracing paper and pencils.

What to do
- Discuss with the children that rainforests are destroyed for timber, space for beef cattle, mining operations and hydroelectric power. Ask them to find out more detail about this destruction and prepare a report using books and the internet.
- Provide a selection of books and articles and a list of or links to useful websites for the children to refer to as they work on their reports.
- When the reports are ready, on screen or paper, let the children present them and/or display them on the classroom wall.

Extension
- Help the children to find a world map at Google Maps™. Ask them to move to the rainforest areas of South America, Africa and south-east Asia and zoom in a little. (Some areas do not have maps at high resolution, so switch to satellite images and let them look at the green of the rainforests below the clouds.)
- Tell the children that it has been estimated that an area of rainforest equal to the size of a football pitch is lost every second. On the UK map, let the children home in on the ground of their favourite team. Ask them to use the satellite pictures to see the rectangle of the pitch surrounded by the ground. Let the children zoom in and, if you have the appropriate licences, print an image of the football ground. Ask them to draw around the pitch on tracing paper, then move the paper every second over the on-screen map to show how areas around the football ground, if they were rainforest, would be destroyed. Point out that this represents the world loss and not how a particular rainforest is cut down.

Did you know?
Many scientists believe that if the rainforests disappear it will get hotter in the Tropics.

IMAGE © M-SAT LTD/SCIENCE PHOTO

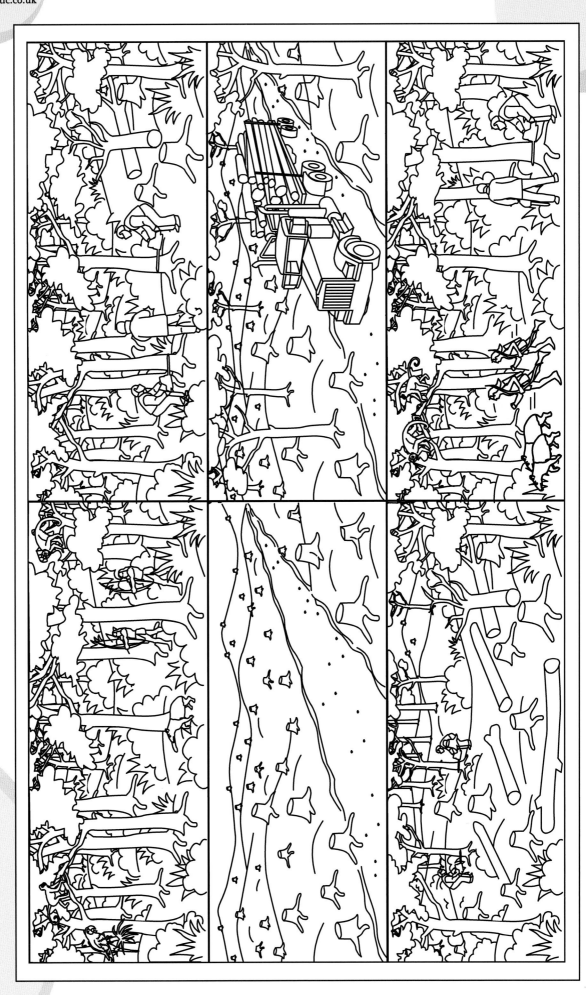

Theme 6 Timber!

Theme 6 Selling it off

SCENE 1

(Stage right is a group of children pretending to be trees. Two MONKEYS swing between the trees. Two MACAWS fly around the trees. A SLOTH moves very slowly, holding on to one tree then stretching out to reach another. Two RAINFOREST PEOPLE gather fruit from the trees.

GOVERNMENT OFFICIALS enter stage left.)

1ST OFFICIAL:	We owe so much money to other countries. Do you think this plan will work?
LEADER:	Of course it will.
2ND OFFICIAL:	We borrowed too much for our schools and hospitals.
1ST OFFICIAL:	But we needed them to help our people have a better chance in life.
2ND OFFICIAL:	You would think the rich countries could help us more. They could say we don't have to pay them back. They have so much more money than us.
LEADER:	Well they don't always do that, so we must see if these people can help us.

(Enter WOOD DEALER and MEAT DEALER)

WOOD DEALER:	Good morning. Thank you for inviting us here. I think we will be able to help you with your problem. I will pay you for all the wood in your forest here and we will take it away to make furniture and paper.
MEAT DEALER:	And when the wood has gone I will pay you to raise cattle on the land. We will use the meat for food in my country.
LEADER:	Excellent! Let us shake hands on it and you can start straight away.

(GOVERNMENT OFFICIALS and DEALERS exit.)

SCENE 2

(All the rainforest trees, animals and people are on stage. Two LUMBERJACKS enter left, carrying chainsaws. They start them up and the MONKEYS and MACAWS flee and exit right. The RAINFOREST PEOPLE shake their fists at the LUMBERJACKS and mime firing arrows at them. Both LUMBERJACKS rev their chainsaws.)

1ST LUMBERJACK: Clear off.

(The RAINFOREST PEOPLE leave through the forest. The SLOTH starts to move slowly, but does not get away before the LUMBERJACKS start work.)

2ND LUMBERJACK: We'll soon have this lot down. You start there and I'll start here.

(LUMBERJACKS cut through the trees and they fall to the floor. They catch up with the SLOTH but ignore it.)

1ST LUMBERJACK: That's our job done. The trucks will be here soon to take this lot away.

Theme 6 Selling it off

SCENE 3

(The two MACAWS fly round the empty stage and depart. The RAINFOREST PEOPLE return and shake their heads. They flee again as a herd of COWS enter. A FARMER behind urges them into the newly cleared forest. The MEAT DEALER returns.)

MEAT DEALER: Look after these cattle with care. Make sure they eat plenty of grass so they can give us plenty of meat.

(MEAT DEALER leaves. COWS moo.)

SCENE 4

Half the number of COWS are on the stage plus the FARMER. 1ST MACAW flies on stage.

1ST MACAW: A few years later.

(The MEAT DEALER enters.)

MEAT DEALER: Why are there fewer cattle?

FARMER: The soil was good at first for growing grass and I could graze plenty of cows. Now the soil has become poor, there is less grass and I cannot graze as many cattle.

MEAT DEALER: Why has the soil changed?

FARMER: The rain has washed it and the goodness away. When the trees were here they kept the soil in place.

MEAT DEALER: We can't have this. I need to supply more meat to my customers.

FARMER: I don't know what you can do.

MEAT DEALER: Ah, but I do.

SCENE 5

(2ND MACAW flies across the stage.)

2ND MACAW: A few weeks later.

(Half the number of COWS are onstage plus the FARMER. The MEAT DEALER and WOOD DEALER enter and turn to face left. The GOVERNMENT OFFICIALS enter.)

MEAT DEALER: Good morning. Thank you for meeting us. We have a problem that I am sure you can help us with.

LEADER: Please tell us.

MEAT DEALER: Your soil doesn't grow as much grass and we can't raise enough cattle. We need some fresh land with better soil.

WOOD DEALER: And I always need plenty of wood.

LEADER: Well I am sure we can help. Let us sell you some more rainforest.

(The other OFFICIALS shake their heads. The LEADER shakes hands with the WOOD DEALER and MEAT DEALER.)

Endangered species

BACKGROUND

The orang-utan is an ape, related to gorillas, chimpanzees and gibbons. The larger of the two species of orang-utan is found in Borneo and the smaller in Sumatra. An orang-utan weighs about 1.5kg at birth and stays with its mother until it is about five or six years old. It then joins a group of orang-utans of the same age. Orang-utans are fully grown at 12 years old and may live until they are 40. Deforestation has been the prime threat to the orang-utan, and now the growth of oil palm plantations prevents rainforests being restored. Orang-utans are seen as pests when they visit these plantations, and are killed.

A living thing becomes extinct if its population becomes so small that it cannot breed fast enough to replace the individuals that die or its habitat is destroyed. Logging, farming and mining, which destroy habitats and endanger species, but there also the effect of human poverty. In the past, people living in rainforests have hunted animals, but only enough for their needs and this has not affected the animals' survival. Today, people travel from overpopulated cities to work in logging camps and on plantations. The wages do not cover their living expenses and the soil lacks minerals for growing food crops. Animals are killed to provide bushmeat which is eaten by local poor people and sold to rich town people as delicacies. Animals are also captured and sold into the pet trade. This is illegal in many countries, but the practice still continues. Orang-utan mothers are shot and their babies taken as pets. The babies are susceptible to human diseases, and perhaps as many as ten die for each one that is sold as a pet.

THE CONTENTS
Lesson 1 (Ages 5–7)
Orang-utans
An account of a day in the life of an orang-utan provides material for testing listening or reading skills and promotes discussion. In the Extension, the children can mime orang-utan movements and make arm extensions to compare their bodies with those of the apes.

Lesson 2 (Ages 7–9)
Animals at risk
The children make masks of a rainforest animal and show there is variation in a species. They take part in an exercise to illustrate extinction and produce maps showing where at-risk animals live.

Lesson 3 (Ages 9–11)
The effects of poverty
The children read and discuss a dialogue between two poor men in Borneo who are contemplating killing and capturing animals for money.

Notes on photocopiables
Orang-utans (page 61)
This fictional report tells of a day in the life of an orang-utan, based on its known activities, which can be used to test listening and reading skills.

Animals at risk (page 62)
These are lists of endangered and vulnerable species in the rainforests of the world. The names of the animals are cut out and used with a map adapted from page 15.

The effects of poverty (page 63)
This is a fictional discussion between two poor people about killing female orang-utans for bushmeat and selling the babies for pets.

IMAGE © ANUDMAN, STOCK.XCHNG

Lesson 1 Orang-utans

IMAGE © MCCONNELL6, STOCK.XCHNG

AGES 5–7

Objectives
● To learn about the daily life of a rainforest animal.
● To understand that the animal is in danger of extinction.

Subject references
English
● Sustain concentration. (NC: KS1 En1 2a)
● Remember specific points that interest them. (NC: KS1 En1 2b)
● Read stories that are challenging in terms of length and vocabulary. (NC: KS1 En2 6f)
Mathematics
● Estimate sizes of objects and compare with standard unit of length. (NC: KS1 Ma3 4a)
Science
● Recognise and compare the main external parts of the bodies of humans and other animals. (NC: KS1 Sc2 2a)

Resources and preparation
● You will need a range of pictures of orang-utans.
● Each child will need a photocopy of page 61 (or you may just need one for yourself to read to the children).
● For the Extension, each child or small group will need: a metre rule, a roll of wallpaper, Blu-Tack®, cardboard (to make arm extensions), scissors.

What to do
● Remind the children of what they discovered about rainforest destruction in Theme 6, Lesson 1. Ask them what they think will happen to the animals and plants in the rainforest if the situation continues. Look for answers about them dying out, and, if appropriate, introduce the word extinction.
● Show the children the pictures of the orang-utans and say that you are going to read them a story about the day in the life of an orang-utan and you are going to ask them questions about it later.
● Read the story to the children (more confident learners may like to read the story

for themselves), and then ask questions relating to the text, such as *When did it get light? How far up the tree was the nest? How did the orang-utans in the rainforest communicate with each other? Why did the orang-utan put a roof on his nest?* Allow the questions and answers to develop into a discussion.

Extension
Tell the children that when a fully grown orang-utan stands upright it is 1.5m tall. Help them to measure and mark out this length on a roll of wallpaper then secure it to the wall so they can compare their own height with the orang-utan's. Go on to tell the children that when a fully grown orang-utan sits down it is 90cm tall. The children can find this measurement on a metre rule. Tell the children to work together to hold the rule vertically and sit next to it to compare their 'sitting down' height. Finally, say that when an orang-utan is standing, its hands reach its ankles. Challenge the children to make some cardboard arm extensions so that they can have arms as long as an orang-utan's.

Lesson 2 Animals at risk

AGES 7–9

Objectives
- To learn that there are individuals within a species.
- To understand the meaning of extinction.
- To know where certain rainforest mammals are at risk.

Subject references
Art and design
- Question and make thoughtful observations about starting points and select ideas to use in their work.
(NC: KS2 1b)
- Collaborate with others on projects in two or three dimensions.
(NC: KS2 5b)

Geography
- Use atlases and maps.
(NC: KS2 2c)

English
- Identify the use and effect of specialist vocabulary.
(NC: KS2 En2 5a)

Resources and preparation
- For the starter, each child will need card to make a mask, scissors, string, sticky tape, coloured pens/pencils/crayons.
- Each child or group will also need photocopies of pages 62 and 15, A3 paper, scissors, glue, coloured pencils. You may want to identify the following areas for less confident learners: Brazil, Costa Rica, Cameroon, Gabon, Central African Republic, Indonesia and Papua New Guinea. For other children, provide a map of the world in an atlas with these areas clearly visible so the children can mark them on their maps.
- You will need a camcorder that can also take still photographs (and permission to film and photograph the children), pictures of rainforest animals.

Starter
Tell the children that when you look at a group of animals, such as a herd of sheep or a flock of pigeons, they all look more-or-less the same, but if you look closer, each one has its own individual markings. It is the same with all animals. Each one is an individual. Ask the children which species of rainforest animal they would like the whole class to pretend to be. Decide on a species, look at pictures of it and let the children

design and make an animal mask. Each one should have some distinguishing markings. When the children have tried on their masks, tell them to set them aside for later.

What to do
- Tell the children that there is a huge number of different kinds of animal in the rainforest, but for this activity they are going to look at animals from one group: mammals. You might also want to say that the activity could be done equally well with other animal groups, such as birds, amphibians, reptiles and insects – all have species that are at risk of dying out.
- Issue the photocopies of pages 15 and page 62. If the children are going to mark in the regions on their maps, issue them with atlases and let them do this now.
- Tell the children that there are three categories into which all endangered living things (including plants) can be placed. The living things are said to be:
– 'critically endangered' if there is an *extremely high* risk of extinction in the wild
– 'endangered' if there is a *very high* risk of extinction in the wild
– 'vulnerable' if there is a *high* risk of extinction in the wild.
- Let the children decide on a colour code

ILLUSTRATION © LASZLO VERES/BEEHIVE ILLUSTRATION

for the categories and colour in the blocks of animals in each category accordingly. The children can then mount their maps on A3 sheets of paper, cut out the blocks of animals and paste them in position around the map. Ask them to use label lines to connect the blocks to the appropriate areas.

Differentiation
● Less confident learners can use maps prepared by you earlier.
● More confident learners can find out about tamarins, marmosets, olingos, mandrills, echidnas, cuscuses and tree kangaroos.

Assessment
The children can be assessed on the quality of their masks and the presentation of their maps.

Plenary
● Ask the children what the maps show. Elicit that there is a large number of animals at risk and that they are found in all rainforest regions.
● Set up a camera so that everyone in the room is in shot, then ask the children to put on their mask and stand up. Tell them that they represent the last population of the animal species and give each child a number. Explain that you are going to take

them back to 1950 – the time when their grandparents may have been born – and will come up to the present time in decades. When a child's number is called out, they should sit down and put their head on the desk. Begin by calling 1950 and numbers 1 to 3, 1960 and numbers 4 to 7, and so on. Increase the numbers so that the species becomes extinct in the present decade.
● Show the children the film and say that some animal species may have become extinct like this in a human lifetime, and that many more are in danger.
● You may wish to use this film as part of a presentation on Rainforest Day.

Outcomes
● The children realise that each animal species is made up of individuals.
● The children learn that many rainforest animals are in varying degrees of risk of extinction.
● The children take part in an activity that illustrates extinction.

Did you know?
Many scientists believe that there are millions of rainforest species still to be discovered.

Lesson 3 The effects of poverty

AGES 9–11

Objectives
● To realise that people can be driven to kill wild animals through poverty.
● To explore ways of solving the bushmeat and pet trade problem through discussion.

Subject references
English
● Identify the gist of an account and evaluate what they hear.
(NC: KS2 En1 2a)
● Make contributions relevant to the topic and take turns in discussion.
(NC: KS2 En1 3a)
● Qualify or justify what they think after listening to others' questions or accounts.
(NC: KS2 En1 3c)
PSHE and citizenship
● Know that resources can be allocated in different ways and that these economic choices can affect individuals, communities and the sustainability of the environment.
(NC: KS2 2j)

IMAGE © BIG_FOOT, STOCK.XCHNG

Resources and preparation
● Each child or group will need a photocopy of page 63.
● For the Extension, you will need information on poverty worldwide.

What to do
● Review Theme 6, Lesson 3 with the children, in which they discussed the exploitation and devastation of rainforests for logging and cattle grazing.
● Remind the children of the animals' habitats that are destroyed, then focus on the fact that there are people in the rainforests too. They are made up of the indigenous tribes who have long made their homes there and people who have moved into the rainforest to work for the logging companies, farms, plantations and mines.
● Tell the children that many people working in the rainforests are very poor and those who have moved into the forests look for ways of earning extra money.
● Issue photocopiable page 63 and let the children read through the transcript. Alternatively, read it to them, or ask three children to take on the roles of the speaking characters while you read the main text.
● When the page has been read, ask the children: *Should the men kill and capture the*

orang-utans? If everyone in class believes the characters should not go hunting, emphasise the plight of the children and try to set up a debate. If necessary, divide the class into halves – for and against – and give them time to prepare their arguments before you debate the issue as a class.
● The children may say that, if their employers won't pay them decently, there should be other ways to earn extra money. You might mention the idea of the hunter becoming the gamekeeper and the area with this wildlife becoming a wildlife sanctuary tourist attraction or safari base. You can develop this further in Theme 9, Lesson 3.

Extension
Let the children use secondary sources such as books, material from charities and the internet to look at world poverty to set rainforest poverty in a broader context. Useful websites are www.poverty.com and www.makepovertyhistory.org.

HOTTOPICS Rainforests

Theme 7 Orang-utans

It is six in the morning and just getting light. Deep in the rainforest is a nest. It is 10m up a tree and is made from leaves and branches. Something is moving inside it. First a hand pokes out and sweeps away one of the large leaves. Then a head pokes out. The orang-utan has woken up.

After a few minutes, he climbs out of the nest and rests on a branch. He smacks his lips together very quickly and the sound spreads through the forest. He listens. After a few moments he hears other lip-smacking sounds. Other orang-utans have woken up and are returning his call.

The orang-utan stands up on the branch and stretches his arms up to grab a branch above him. With one foot in front of the other, he slowly makes his way along the branch. He holds on to the branch above to keep him from falling.

On a thin, springy part of the branch, he starts to move up and down. The branch dips under his weight and he starts to swing backwards and forwards. He makes a big swing then lets go of the branch and flies through the air as if he had been shot out of a catapult. He reaches the next tree and grabs a branch. His grip is firm and the branch is strong. He is safe.

The orang-utan rests for a moment, then swings through the branches to a place where figs are growing. He sits on a branch among the figs and has a long breakfast.

At midday he finds a nest he made a few days ago and climbs in for a nap. After an hour a sound wakes him up. It is coming from the ground below him. He looks through the leaves and sees people. They have cameras and binoculars and are looking up at him. The orang-utan smacks his lips loudly and breaks off branches around him. He throws them at the people below and they move away.

He swings through more branches, then finds some more food. His meal this time is mangoes. Later, he finds a gap in the branches that he cannot swing across, so he carefully climbs down a tree trunk to the ground. He looks around, then walks on his hands and feet to another tree. Slowly, he climbs the trunk and then, after a rest, swings on through the branches.

By six in the evening it is dark again and the orang-utan has made another nest. It has a platform of branches to lie on and a roof like an umbrella to keep off the rain. He roars before he settles down and hears another orang-utan roar back to him across the forest. Soon there is a heavy shower of rain, but the orang-utan is asleep and dry in his nest.

Theme 7 Animals at risk

BRAZIL

Critically endangered
 Black-faced lion tamarin
 Golden-rumped lion tamarin
 Capuchin monkey

Endangered
 Buffy-headed marmoset
 Giant otter
 Golden-headed lion tamarin
 Golden lion tamarin
 Pied tamarin
 Maned three-toed sloth
 White-whiskered spider monkey

Vulnerable
 Black-headed marmoset
 Blackish squirrel monkey
 Brown howler monkey
 Bokermann's nectar bat
 Brazilian big-eyed bat

COSTA RICA

Endangered
 Harris's olingo
 Red-backed squirrel monkey

Vulnerable
 Central american tapir
 Giant anteater
 Lemurine night monkey
 Grey woolly monkey
 Lowland woolly monkey
 Long-haired spider monkey
 Golden-white tassel-ear marmoset

CAMEROON

Endangered
 Chimpanzee
 Crested genet
 Drill
 Preuss's monkey

Vulnerable
 African elephant
 Black colobus
 Mandrill

GABON

Endangered
 Chimpanzee
 Drill
 Western gorilla

Vulnerable
 African elephant
 Mandrill
 Sun-tailed monkey

CENTRAL AFRICAN REPUBLIC

Endangered
 Chimpanzee
 Gorilla
 Red colobus

INDONESIA

Critically endangered
 Javan rhinoceros
 Mentawai macaque
 Silvery gibbon
 Sumatran flying squirrel
 Sumatran orang-utan
 Sumatran rhinoceros

Endangered
 Black-spotted cuscus
 Celebes black macaque
 Moor macaque
 Grizzled leaf monkey
 Pig-tailed snub-nosed monkey
 Proboscis monkey
 Bornean orang-utan
 Long-beaked echidna
 Tiger

PAPUA NEW GUINEA

Endangered
 Black-spotted cuscus
 Telefomin cuscus
 Fergusson Island striped possum
 Goodfellow's tree-kangaroo
 Huon tree-kangaroo
 Long-beaked echidna

Theme 7 The effects of poverty

(There is a group of huts by a road. Around them the land is just bare soil and tree stumps. In the far distance on the left are the remains of the rainforest that has yet to be cut down. On the right is an oil palm plantation. Close to the huts some food crops have been planted, but they are not thriving. A man called Dahari sits on the step of his hut. His wife looks after their two small children who are not well. A second man, Lokman, comes out of his hut next door. His wife goes to look at the crops they have planted to find something to eat. Their two children help her.)

Lokman:	I've heard there are a group of orang-utans along the road; in that clump of trees the loggers will take next week. Are you coming to get them?'
Dahari:	I don't know. I don't like it. They should just pay us more.
Lokman:	The loggers you mean? Well, they promised us a good wage when we left the city, but they didn't keep their word.
Dahari:	No, and then we couldn't afford to go back.
Lokman:	You tried working on the plantation.
Dahari:	And their pay was just as bad.
Lokman:	Come on, we have no choice. Get those sticks and twine and help me make some cages. Sri has lent me his gun so we can shoot the mothers for meat and you can cage up the babies.
Dahari:	I don't know... they look too human.
Lokman:	But their meat is good and what we don't eat we can sell, and you can use the money to get medicines for your kids. Come on, we've shot and eaten other animals. They're no different.

(Dahari's children start to wail from inside the hut. His wife comes to the door and looks at him for help. Dahari gathers the sticks and twine and begins making the cages.
Lokman goes to his hut and brings out a machete and cleans it.

An old lorry comes bumping along the road. It stops outside the huts and a man leans out of the window.)

Driver:	Hey Lokman, there's a fine group of orangs up the road. I've got some stuff to pick up further along, but when I come back I can take all the bush meat you can sell me. There look to be about six babies that should do well at the pet dealers.
Lokman:	We're just getting ready. Dahari isn't keen though. He thinks things might get better. Ha ha.
Driver:	Dahari, you dreamer, get those cages finished and get them on your cart. There aren't many orangs left around here. Better get them while you can.

(The lorry trundles along the ruts in the road. Lokman brings the cart from the back of his hut and Dahari loads it with the finished cages. Lokman gathers up his rifle and machete. Dahari looks up at his wife and she smiles back at him. Lokman is already striding out up the road and Dahari pushes the cart after him.)

Rainforest benefits

BACKGROUND

Many rainforest plants provide us with food, medicines and other useful materials. Food from rainforest plants includes banana, mango, avocado, pineapple, sweet potato, star fruit, passion fruit, Brazil nuts, cashew nuts, sugar, chocolate and cocoa, coffee, tea, vanilla, lime, orange, lemon, grapefruit, tangerine, pineapple, tapioca. Spices include: nutmeg, ginger, clove, cinnamon, black pepper, chilli pepper, turmeric, paprika. The rainforest also provides: camphor, used in insect repellents; rubber; rattan (furniture and baskets); ramie (canvas, clothes and commercial fishing nets); jute (ropes and flooring); hessian (curtains and carpets); bamboo (furniture and garden products); rosewood (to make furniture and to treat skin conditions such as acne); and sandalwood (in perfume and soaps). The following are not featured on the worksheets in this theme, but you might like to add them to the lesson: quinine, used in the treatment of malaria, and curare, used in surgery to relax muscles.

THE CONTENTS
Lesson 1 (Ages 5–7)
Rainforest foods

The children examine data from a fictitious survey and convert it from a table to a pictogram. They hold their own class survey.

Lesson 2 (Ages 7–9)
Rainforest products

The children learn about the foods and materials that come from plants that originally grew or continue to grow in the rainforest.

Lesson 3 (Ages 9–11)
Rainforests and the world

The children take an extended look at rainforest foods and products. In the Extension, they consider how removing the rainforest reduces the chance of finding new products and adversely affects our planet's environment.

Notes on photocopiables
Rainforest foods (page 69)

This made-up data represents how many people in a class have eaten (or eat regularly) certain foods from rainforest origin. Symbols of rainforest trees are provided to cut out and use in a pictogram from the data.

Rainforest products (page70)

This sheet contains labels for 36 products that are derived from rainforest plants.

Rainforests and the world (page 71)

This information text shows how the rainforest affects the amount of carbon dioxide in the air and water in the environment. The answers are: 1) A gas that makes the atmosphere behave like greenhouse glass; 2) From the Sun to the inside of the greenhouse; 3) They stop heat from the Earth passing out into space; 4) By the burning of coal, oil, gas and petrol; 5) It makes it rise because the burning wood releases carbon dioxide, and trees, which take up carbon dioxide, are removed; 6) The plants would take up more carbon dioxide. It could slow down global warming. 7) More water runs away from the area, less evaporates and condenses to form clouds, when it rains again more water runs away and even less water is left to evaporate.

IMAGE © BLUEGUM, STOCK.XCHNG

Lesson 1 Rainforest foods

IMAGE © NOTA, STOCK.XCHNG

Resources and preparation
- Each child or group will need: a photocopy of page 69, scissors, glue, access to computers.
- You will also need: a banana, mango, avocado, pineapple and sweet potato.
- For the Extension, you will need: samples of nutmeg, ginger, cloves and cinnamon.

What to do
- Ask the children to name some of the foods that they eat. Steer them away from prepared products to the foods they are made from, and to fruits, vegetables and even spices. Find out and make a quick tally of how many eat, for example, apples, oranges and potatoes.
- Tell the children that some foods that they eat come from rainforest plants. Show them your collection of rainforest foods. Say what each one is and perhaps let the children handle and smell them, particularly if any are unfamiliar. Tell the children that a group of people were asked if they ate any of these foods and the results have been collected on the sheet – hand out the photocopies of page 69.
- Go through the table with the children, relating the food names to the real examples you have collected. Then tell them that you would like them to make a pictogram of the results by cutting out the correct number of trees and sticking them in the correct places on the blank chart at the bottom of the sheet.
- Then hold a survey of the class to find out who has eaten (or eats regularly)

each of the five items. Collect the data on the board, then let the children make pictograms of the class results. If possible, set up this exercise so the pictogram can be created on computer.

Extension
- Tell the children that chocolate (cocoa), sugar, cashew nuts, Brazil nuts and coffee also come from rainforest plants. Conduct another survey and let the children prepare the results for display, using ICT. Encourage them to compare the results of the two surveys and draw conclusions on which types of rainforest foods their class members eat most.
- Show the children the samples of rainforest spices: nutmeg, ginger, cloves and cinnamon, and talk about how they are used to give flavour to foods.

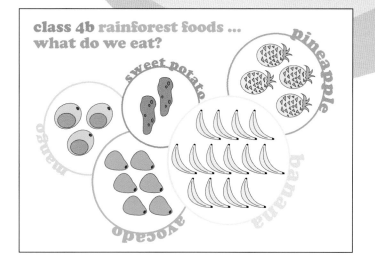

class 4b rainforest foods ...
what do we eat?

AGES 5–7

Objectives
- To become aware that some common and less common foods come from rainforest plants.
- To use, interpret and present data.

Subject references
Science
(NC: KS1 Sc1 2g)
Communicate what happened in a variety of ways including ICT.
- Know that humans need food to stay alive.
(NC: KS1 Sc2 2a)
- Use their senses to recognise the similarities and differences between materials.
(NC: KS1 Sc3 1a)
Mathematics
- Solve a relevant problem by using tables and charts to sort out and organise information.
(NC: KS1 Ma2 5a)
ICT
- Present their completed work effectively.
(NC: KS1 3b)

Lesson 2 Rainforest products

Objectives
• To be able to collect and display data using mathematical processes.
• To learn about useful products from the rainforest.
• To know that the rainforest is a valuable resource for humans.

Subject references
Mathematics
• Select and use data-handling skills when solving problems.
(NC: KS2 Ma4 1a)
• Represent discrete data using bar charts, using ICT when appropriate.
(NC: KS2 Ma4 2c)
Art and design
• Make thoughtful observations about starting points and select ideas for use in their work.
(NC: KS2 1b)
• Collect visual information to help them develop their ideas.
(NC: KS2 1c)
ICT
• Develop and refine ideas by bringing together, organising and reorganising text and images.
(NC: KS2 2a)

Resources and preparation
• Each child or small group will need: a photocopy of page 70, paper (including A3 size), pens, access to a wide variety of secondary sources such as books and websites and food magazines (for cutting out pictures), computer access.
• You may like to show examples of some or all of the items listed on page 70 (except nuts)

Starter
Ask the children if they have eaten or drunk anything from the rainforest today. When they look puzzled, tell them that tea, coffee and cocoa all come from plants that originally grew in the rainforest. Repeat the question.

What to do
• Issue the photocopies of page 70 and go through the items with the children. If you have examples of some of the items, hold them up as you go though the list. Point out anything (for example something made from rubber) that is not in its original form.
• Give the children some time to read the list again and decide which of the food items they eat. Work together as a class to produce a frequency table on the board, then let the children construct bar charts to show how many children eat each product listed. Alternatively, organise the class to work as four groups to collect and display

their individual data. Then let each group compare their data with that of other groups.
• Tell the children that the rainforest has provided us with many things we use today. Some plants have provided us with substances that can be used as medicines for the treatment of conditions such as asthma, bronchitis and certain cancers, and there is evidence that there are plants in the forests that could provide us with more useful materials, including further medicinal substances. The problem is, however, that we are destroying the rainforest so fast that scientists cannot even identify all the potentially useful plants, let alone ensure they are saved. Within the tribes of the rainforests there are shamans or 'medicine men' who do know the healing powers of many of the rainforest plants. Their knowledge is not written down, but passed down from one generation to the next. As the rainforests are destroyed and the tribes are forced to move out, the knowledge of the shaman is lost when these displaced generations die.
• Ask the children to make a poster, on paper and/or on screen, to encourage people to want to save the rainforest and recognise that it is a source of useful things. Explain that they do not have to mention all the items listed on the sheet, but they should make a selection that they think will contribute to conveying their message.

- Let the children work on their own or in small groups and use secondary sources and materials to construct their poster.

Differentiation

- Less confident learners will need help with the construction of bar graphs and the selection of items for their poster.
- More confident learners may like to consider that tribes need to be able to live in the rainforests. Not just because they have the right to stay in their homes, but so that the shamans can continue their work of passing on their information. This can then be shared with scientists so new beneficial substances can be found to help cure diseases worldwide.

Assessment

The children can be assessed by the accuracy of their bar graphs and the effectiveness of their posters.

Plenary

Let the children display their posters on the wall and discuss how well they convey the idea that the rainforests should be saved because they are a useful resource for everyone.

Outcomes

- The children can collect and display information using tables and bar graphs.
- They can make a poster to show that the rainforest is a valuable resource that is worth saving.

Did you know?

Some rainforest people keep bees and silkworms to provide us with honey and silk.

POLAROID IMAGES: TOP © TAMAFANTA, STOCK.XCHNG; MIDDLE © SCYZA, STOCK.XCHNG; BOTTOM © IRKATA, STOCK.XCHNG

ILLUSTRATION © LASZLO VERES/BEEHIVE ILLUSTRATION

Lesson 3 Rainforests and the world

AGES 9–11

Objectives
● To learn about useful products from the rainforest.
● To learn that the removal of the rainforest can produce changes in the Earth's environment.

Subject references
Mathematics
● Select and use data-handling skills when solving problems.
(NC: KS2 Ma4 1a)
● Construct frequency tables.
(NC: KS2 Ma4 2b)
● Represent discrete data using bar charts, using ICT when appropriate.
(NC: KS2 Ma4 2c)

English
● Obtain specific information through detailed reading.
(NC: KS2 En2 3c)
● Review and comment on what has been read, seen or heard.
(NC: KS2 En3 9d)

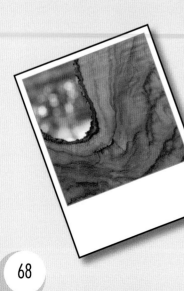

Resources and preparation
● Each child or group will need: photocopies of pages 70, and 71 (for the Extension), paper, pens, a selection of products (except nuts) from those featured on page 70.

What to do
● Tell the children that some of the plants found in the rainforest provide us with food and other useful substances and materials. Most of these plants are now not directly harvested from the rainforest but specially grown on farms and plantations.
● Issue photocopiable page 70 and let the children read through the list of names. Use the information in the background notes to tell them about the use of the less familiar ones such as camphor, rattan, bamboo, rosewood, sandalwood, jute and ramie.
● Tell the children to tick each food that is used in their home. This exercise can be extended for homework by letting the children find out about rainforest foods used in the homes of other members of their family – aunts, uncles, grandparents and so on – to discover how widely these foods are used. A further extension would be to find out which homes have furniture or other

products made of rosewood, rattan (cane) and bamboo.
● Work as a class, or let the children work in groups, to pool their results using frequency tables. Then ask them to display the data as bar graphs.

Extension
● Having established that rainforest plants have made a large contribution to our diet and, to some extent, house furnishings, for example, move on to discuss how the rainforests affect other aspects of our world. Issue photocopiable page 71, which provides brief information about greenhouse gases and how rainforests absorb carbon dioxide and help to control water flow. Let the children read the text and answer the questions.
● Go through the answers. Then, ask the children to recall all their work so far and to prepare a paragraph on why they think that rainforests should be saved. This could be developed into a more focused and extended exercise on persuasive writing.

Theme 8 Rainforest foods

Food	Number of people who eat it
banana	8
mango	3
avocado	4
pineapple	6
sweet potato	2

Number of people

banana   mango   avocado   pineapple   sweet potato

Theme 8 They came from the rainforest

Coconut	Brazil nut	Cashew nut	Avocado
Sweet potato	Coffee	Tea	Cocoa
Chocolate	Sugar	Vanilla	Cinnamon
Lime	Orange	Lemon	Grapefruit
Tangerine	Banana	Mango	Pineapple
Varnish	Orchids	Black pepper	Allspice
Christmas cactus	Chilli pepper	Cloves	Ginger
Nutmeg	Turmeric	Paprika	Tapioca
Camphor	Rubber	Rattan	Bamboo
Rosewood	Sandalwood	Jute	Ramie

Theme 8 Rainforests and the world

Carbon dioxide

Many scientists agree that the world's climate is changing due to global warming. The increase in temperature is due to an increase in "greenhouse gases". These are gases which make the atmosphere behave like glass in a greenhouse. Greenhouse glass lets heat from the Sun pass through it, but does not let heat from inside the greenhouse pass out. In a similar way, air with lots of greenhouse gases in it lets heat from the Sun reach the Earth, but does not let heat from the Earth escape into space. This makes conditions on the Earth warmer.

Carbon dioxide is a greenhouse gas. For a long time, large amounts of carbon dioxide have been released into the air by the burning of coal and oil. This is continuing today, together with the burning of large amounts of natural gas and petrol.

Plants use carbon dioxide in the air to make food. They take it into their leaves when the Sun shines on them and, in a process called photosynthesis, they use the carbon in the carbon dioxide to make substances that the plant needs. Large amounts of the carbon that the plants take in is used to make their bodies. A plant can be thought of as a carbon store.

When a section of rainforests is cut down, the tree trunks are taken away and used for furniture or paper, but most of the branches are burnt. The carbon in it is changed to carbon dioxide which returns to the air.

Water

Plants use water to make food too. They only use up a little of the water they take in through their roots. Most of the water evaporates from their leaves, and this gives the plant power to pull water up through its stem. In a rainforest, evaporated water rises in the air, condenses and forms clouds. The clouds give the rainforest shade from the Sun, then storms develop and the clouds release rain back onto the plants. When the water reaches the ground it is quickly taken up by the plant roots.

When a rainforest is cut down, fewer clouds develop. The land below them and the forests around them become hotter than normal. Less rain falls, so the climate is drier, which makes it difficult for any remaining plants to survive. When that rain does fall there are few roots to take it up, so it runs away carrying the soil with it. The soil gets into rivers and blocks them. As the water rises, it floods the surrounding areas.

1. What is a greenhouse gas?
2. Which way does heat pass through greenhouse glass?
3. Why do greenhouse gases make the Earth warmer?
4. How have large amounts of carbon dioxide in the air been produced?
5. How does the destruction of rainforests affect the amount of carbon dioxide in the air? Explain your answer.
6. What would be the effect of planting rainforest where it has been destroyed?
7. How does removing a rainforest alter the water cycle?

Saving the rainforests

BACKGROUND

Huge areas of rainforest have been lost and others are being destroyed at a rapid rate, but there are still very large areas that could be saved. Some estimates suggest that, at the current rate of destruction, all the rainforests could be gone by the mid-twentifirst century. While a simple reason for saving the rainforest is habitat conservation, the previous theme has shown that rainforests also provide valuable products and medicines. The loss of rainforests could affect the global climate and make rainforest people homeless. The reasons for rainforest destruction are financial, as highlighted in Theme 6, Lesson 2. Keeping the rainforests must therefore offer financial rewards. People who work for logging companies and sell bushmeat could perhaps earn a living through eco-tourism instead. They could become guides, game wardens or hotel/camp staff. Many rainforest tribes have no land ownership and are nomadic. They have come to grow single crops for money, which quickly destroys the soil's mineral content. If governments gave tribal people entitlement to plots of land, they could settle, grow mixtures of crops and manage the soil better. Selectively removing large trees and leaving others to grow in their place is one way of harvesting rainforest wood without damaging the forest. Another way is to set up plantations in areas that have already been cleared. Harvesting from there means that the rainforest does not have to be damaged further at all.

THE CONTENTS

Lesson 1 (Ages 5–7)
Rescuing the rainforest

The children learn a song about how to save the rainforests and work out how to perform it in an amusing and educational manner.

Lesson 2 (Ages 7–9)
Good idea, bad idea

The children imagine that they are living on an island where there is a rainforest. Before the loggers continue logging, the islanders gather to consider other ways to earn money.

Lesson 3 (Ages 9–11)
Rainforest conservation

The children imagine that they are government officials set the task of conserving a rainforest, yet still making it earn an income for its people.

Notes on photocopiables
Rescuing the rainforest (page 77)

This song is written for descant recorders (two or three) and untuned percussion such as a drum or maracas. The chant should start as a whisper and grow to a shout at the end. The percussion should begin quietly and get louder too. The children could stand in two groups for this performance: a group of two or three to sing the solo bars and a larger group to join in with the rest.

Good idea, bad idea (page 78)

Here is a range of ideas for rainforest conservation for the children to consider.

Rainforest conservation (page 79)

This map shows an island which is mostly covered in rainforest, although some has been destroyed. The children choose a site for a hotel and a path through the rainforest for tourists to travel.

IMAGE © PAPALEGUAS, STOCK.XCHNG

Lesson 1 Rescuing the rainforest

PHOTOGRAPH © PETER ROWE

AGES 5–7

Objectives
● To learn the words and tune to a song and perform it.
● To work out and perform actions to accompany the song.

Subject references
Music
● Use voices expressively by singing songs and speaking chants.
(NC: KS1 1a)
● Explore and express their ideas and feelings about music using movement and dance.
(NC: KS1 3a)
● Understand how music is used for a particular purpose.
(NC: KS1 4d)
● Work as a class.
(NC: KS1 5c)
Physical education
● Use movement imaginatively, responding to stimuli, including music, and performing basic skills.
(NC: KS1 6a)

Resources and preparation
● Each child or group will need a photocopy of page 77.
● You will need pictures of the animals referred to in the song (frog, tapir, jaguar, monkey, snake), and you may want material for props (for the Extension).
● You may wish to integrate this song with the play 'Selling it off' in Theme 6, Lesson 2. The song could follow on from the play to lighten the mood and offer hope. You may also want the children to perform their song in costume as part of Rainforest Day (see Planning a project, on page 6).

What to do
● Tell the children that they are going to learn a song about rescuing the rainforest. As you go through the lyrics, remind the children about their previous studies. Encourage them to look at pictures of the animals mentioned and think about how rainforests are destroyed.
● If you have not mentioned poaching before, you should do so now. At this level you could simply say that people hunt animals not just for their own food but to sell to others (bushmeat). Explain that some people also capture animals to sell as exotic pets. Remind the children of the green belt of rainforest around the Earth they looked at in Theme 1, Lesson 1.

● Teach the children the song and rehearse it for a performance.

Extension
Discuss with the children how they could make the song more visually entertaining. For example:
– During the chant, raise trees made from poles and cardboard across the back of the stage.
– For verse 1, line 1, the children hold up cut-out frog faces and throw buckets of blue paper water into the air. For line 2, one child struts like a tapir and another stalks like jaguar. For line 3, children climb like monkeys or slide like snakes.
– Throughout verse 3, the trees are lowered until at the last line all are down. In line 1, children mime chopping and sawing; some of the trees at the back fall. Line 2, children as birds fly away. Line 3, children mime loading logs and starting fires. Last line, children point to fallen trees.
– During each of the first two lines of verse 3, the children simply put up their hands to signal stop. Line 3, children mime scattering seeds and pointing to the back as all the trees rise again. Last line, two children come on stage with a large beach ball or globe, turning it to show the green band of the rainforests.

Lesson 2 Good idea, bad idea

Resources and preparation
● Each group will need a photocopy of page 78.
● You will need pictures of rainforest animals and people, pictures of people in hospital, a selection of rainforest food and products.

Starter
Show the children and talk about the pictures of rainforest animals and people and the rainforest products. Then show the children the images of people in hospital and say that many plants in the rainforests have substances in them that we can use as medicines to fight disease. After this discussion, ask the children to think of what they would say to someone to encourage them to help you save the rainforests. What good reasons for their conservation can they give?

What to do
● Organise the children to work in groups of four.
● Tell the children (or remind them if you have worked on Theme 6, Lesson 2) that rainforests are cut down to make people money from logging, cattle grazing, palm growing or mining.
● Ask the children to imagine that they are living on an island where there is a rainforest. Some of it has been removed already, but before the loggers continue chopping down the trees, the people of the island (the children's group) gather to consider other ways they might be able to make money from the rainforest, in a more sustainable way.
● Issue the photocopies of page 78 and tell the children that it suggests some ideas to

IMAGE © LLANDUDNO, STOCK.XCHNG

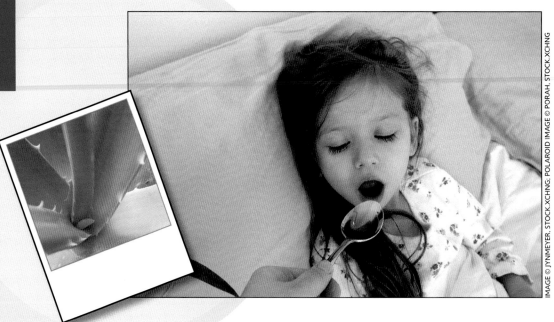

IMAGE © JYNMEYER, STOCK.XCHNG; POLAROID IMAGE © PORAH, STOCK.XCHNG

consider in deciding what to do about the rainforest crisis. Point to the village on the map where the islanders live and encourage the children to note the extent of the logging so far. If the logging were to continue removing rainforest, what might happen to the island and islanders eventually?

- Give the groups time to work out, discuss and agree on a plan they think would work to save the rainforest and at the same time earn enough money for the people to live on.
- Encourage the children to think about how one idea may affect another. For example, hunting a few animals for food may seem like a good idea as this is what rainforest tribes have done for thousands of years. However, is it sustainable on a large scale and over the long term? If people earn money at the hotel, they can spend it on importing meat from farm animals. Also, if the tourists were to find out that hunting was still practised, they may feel that the island was not really committed to conservation of all species and may not return. Tell or remind the children that keeping (and selling) protected animals as pets is also illegal.

Differentiation

- Less confident learners may need help in understanding how the hotel and growing a mixture of crops may help people and the rainforest.
- More confident learners could consider how they would apportion the land for people to grow crops for themselves and what laws that they would make up and enforce to prevent the trade in bushmeat and exotic pets.

Assessment

The children could be assessed on the contributions they make in the group debates.

ILLUSTRATION © LASZLO VERES/BEEHIVE ILLUSTRATION; POLAROID IMAGES © KMG, STOCK.XCHNG

Plenary

Ask each group to report its conclusions to the class. If there are differences of opinion between groups, let the debate continue at class level until a whole class 'policy' is established. You may like to introduce a voting system to produce the policy democratically.

Outcomes

- The children have considered the economics involved in rainforest conservation.
- The children have taken part in a debate and made a democratic decision.

Lesson 3 Rainforest conservation

AGES 9–11

Objectives
● To think about how rainforests can be conserved.
● To develop a strategy for rainforest conservation, through debate.
● To explore strategies to encourage people to support rainforest conservation.

Subject references
English
● Identify the key points in a discussion and evaluate what they hear.
(NC: KS2 En2 2a)
● Ask relevant questions to clarify, extend and follow up ideas.
(NC: KS2 En2 2b)
● Respond to others appropriately, taking into account what they say.
(NC: KS2 En2 2e)
● Persuade, focusing on how arguments and evidence are built up and language used to convince a reader.
(NC: KS2 En3 9c)
PSHE and citizenship
● Discuss and debate topical issues.
(NC: KS2 2a)
● Know that resources can be allocated in different ways and that these economic choices affect individuals, communities and the sustainability of the environment.
(NC: KS2 2j)

Resources and preparation
● Each group will need a photocopy of page 79, coloured pencils. You may also like to provide photocopies of page 78 to act as a stimulus for debate.
● For the Extension, the children will need paper and pens and/or computers with internet access.

What to do
● Organise the children into small groups.
● Ask the children to imagine that they are officials working for a country's government and have been given the task of conserving a rainforest in one of the country's islands. Advise them that, at the moment, logging of the rainforest is taking place. The local people are growing some rice in the cleared area to sell. They are also hunting wild animals in the forest to sell as bushmeat and in the pet trade. The officials' challenge is to develop a plan to present to the islanders that will ensure that the rainforest is conserved without loss to the island people's livelihood. The main proposal is that a hotel or lodge will be built and a path cleared and maintained that can take tourists on guided treks through the rainforest.

● Let the children discuss the problems and potential solutions in their groups and then present their ideas to the class for debate. Tell them that in their plans they should consider where the hotel or eco-lodge might be built, if sustainable logging (cutting down a few big trees) is to continue and where it should take place, what features the path should pass, the possible site of a gift shop and methods of enforcing a ban on trade in bushmeat and pets. Let the children mark up and annotate the map.

Extension
● The children could design posters or write persuasive speeches to encourage people to support rainforest conservation.
● They may like to take their involvement further to adopt a part of a rainforest as described at www.rainforest-alliance.org. Click on the 'adopt a rainforest' link.

Did you know?
If the soil is not lost when a rainforest is cleared it can grow back in a hundred years.

IMAGE © IMAGEBROKER/ALAMY

Theme 9 Rescuing the rainforest

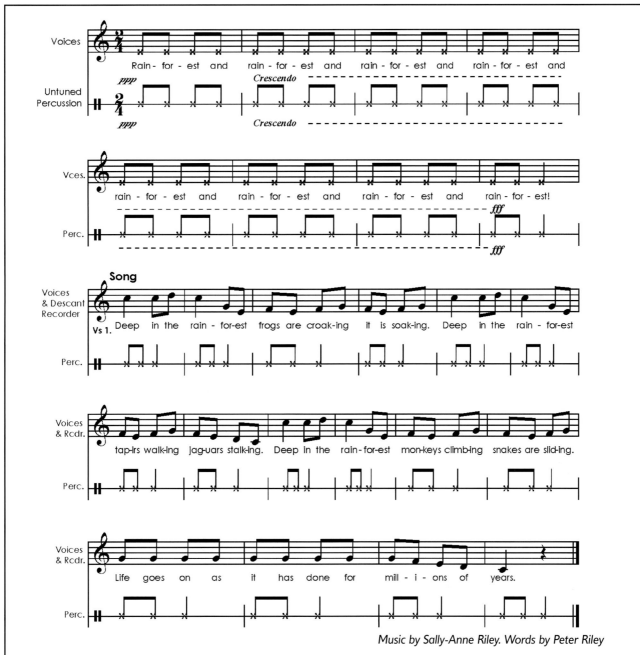

Music by Sally-Anne Riley. Words by Peter Riley

VERSE 1

(one or two singers)
Deep in the rainforest –
frogs are croaking, it is soaking.
Deep in the rainforest –
tapirs walking, jaguars stalking.
Deep in the rainforest – monkeys
climbing, snakes are sliding.
(all)
Life goes on
As it has done
For millions of years.

VERSE 2

(one or two singers)
Inside the rainforest –
men are chopping, men are sawing.
Inside the rainforest – trees are
falling, birds are calling.
Inside the rainforest – logs are
loading, fires are burning.
(all)
The jungle's gone.
There's nowhere left
For anything to live.

VERSE 3

(one or two singers)
Let's help the rainforest – stop the
cutting and the felling.
Let's help the rainforest – stop the
poaching, farms encroaching.
Let's help the rainforest – start
some sowing, keep them growing.
(all)
So once again
A belt of green
Can grow around the Earth.

Theme 9 Good idea, bad idea

Theme 9 Rainforest conservation

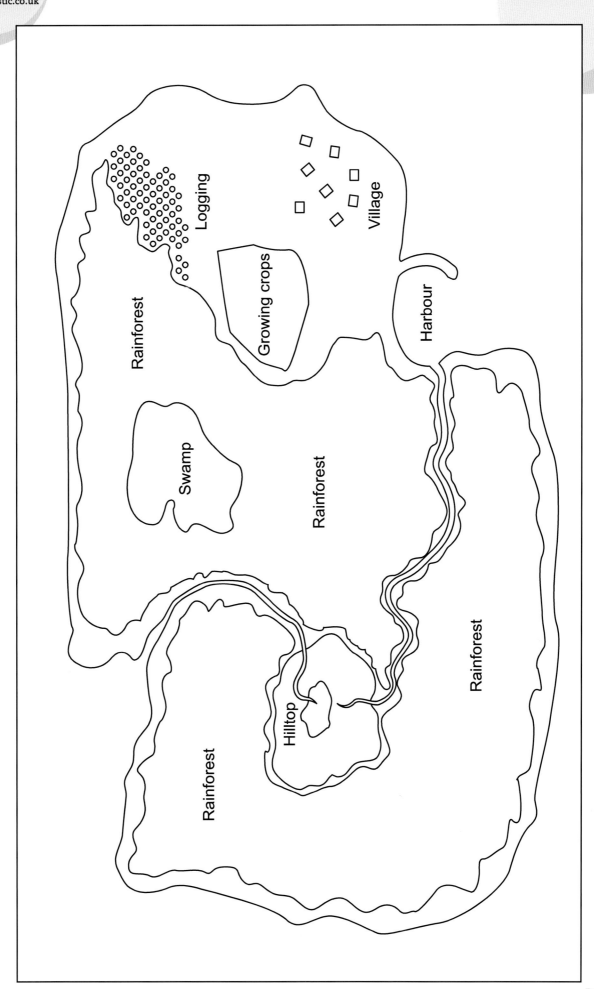

Logging

Village

Rainforest

Growing crops

Harbour

Swamp

Rainforest

Rainforest

Hilltop

Rainforest

SCHOLASTIC

In this series:

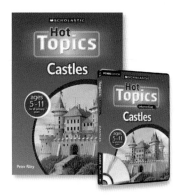

978-0439-94510-3 (Book)
978-1407-12232-8 (CD-ROM)

978-0439-94509-7 (Book)
978-1407-12233-5 (CD-ROM)

978-0439-94511-0 (Book)
978-1407-12234-2 (CD-ROM)

978-0439-94573-8 (Book)
978-1407-12235-9 (CD-ROM)

978-0439-94552-3 (Book)
978-1407-12236-6 (CD-ROM)

978-0439-94574-5 (Book)
978-1407-12238-0 (CD-ROM)

ISBN 978-0439-94553-0 (Book)
978-1407-12237-3 (CD-ROM)

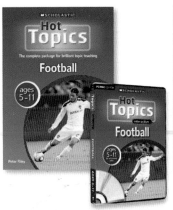

978-1407-12710-1 (Book)
978-1407-12714-9 (CD-ROM)

978-1407-12713-2 (Book)
978-1407-12717-0 (CD-ROM)

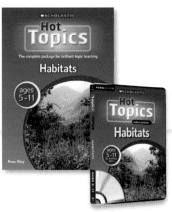

978-1407-12712-5 (Book)
978-1407-12716-3 (CD-ROM)

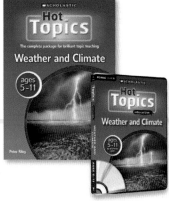

978-1407-12711-8 (Book)
978-1407-12715-6 (CD-ROM)

To find out more, call: **0845 603 9091**
or visit **www.scholastic.co.uk**